RUSSIAN AIRCRAFT
OF THE COLD WAR
1945–90

RUSSIAN AIRCRAFT OF THE COLD WAR
1945–90

EDWARD WARD

First published in 2025

Copyright © 2025 Amber Books Ltd

All rights reserved. No part of this publication may be reproduced, stored in a retrieval system, or transmitted in any form or by any means, electronic, mechanical, photocopying, recording, or otherwise, without prior written permission of the copyright holder.

Published by Amber Books Ltd
United House
London N7 9DP
United Kingdom
www.amberbooks.co.uk
Facebook: amberbooks
YouTube: amberbooksltd
Instagram: amberbooksltd
X(Twitter): @amberbooks

ISBN: 978-1-83886-471-2

Editor: Michael Spilling
Designers: Ummagumma and Mark Batley
Picture research: Terry Forshaw

Printed in China

Contents

Introduction	6
Fighters	8
Attack Aircraft	46
Bombers	60
Reconnaissance, Electronic Warfare and Utility	78
Transport	90
Helicopters	106
INDEX	125
PICTURE CREDITS	128

Introduction

At times the world's most powerful national air arm during the Cold War period, Soviet military aviation advanced from a somewhat disadvantaged position in 1945 to become a behemoth in terms of both capability and technology, until the nation it served and defended ceased to exist in 1991.

When World War II ended, the Soviet Union was in possession of the world's most powerful tactical air arm consisting of fighter, attack and bombing aircraft that were amongst the best fielded by any nation. However, in the fields of strategic bombing capability, jet engine propulsion and naval aviation, the USSR lagged behind the other Allied powers.

Nonetheless, within three years of the end of the war the Soviets were flying a long-range nuclear-capable bomber, in the form of the Tupolev Tu-4, and arguably the best fighter aircraft in the world, the Mikoyan-Gurevich MiG-15, an aircraft with such a spectacular performance that it had only one viable rival worldwide, the North American F-86 Sabre. Both Soviet aircraft were made possible by the acquisition of Western technology – by luck, purchase, or theft – with Boeing B-29s that had crash-landed in the USSR providing a model for the Tu-4, and British Rolls-Royce Nene jet engines that had been bought in 1946, and subsequently copied, in the case of the MiG-15. What is remarkable, however, is that after entering the Cold

The MiG-17 'Fresco' showed unexpected success during the Vietnam War when combatting American fighters such as the F-4 Phantom and F-105 Thunderchief.

INTRODUCTION

A flight of Ilyushin Il-28 'Beagles'. More than 6000 of this very successful type were built, with many being operated by Warsaw Pact allies such as Poland, Czechoslovakia and East Germany.

War at something of a disadvantage, the Soviets then continued to develop aviation technology at a speed that kept pace with the West and regularly exceeded it.

Distinct arms

Throughout the Cold War, the Soviet Air Force, *Voenno-Vozdushnye Sily,* or 'VVS', was split into distinct and separate air arms. By far the largest was 'Frontal Aviation', which included all tactical fighters, bombers, attack and reconnaissance aircraft.

Strategic combat aircraft came under the control of 'Long Range Aviation' operating heavy bombers, long range reconnaissance and inflight refuelling tankers.

'Military Transport Aviation' dealt with transport aircraft (though Frontal Aviation also included a transport element) and 'Army Aviation', which operated aircraft in direct support of ground troops, mainly in the form of helicopters.

In addition, the Soviet Air Defence Forces, *Voyska Protivovozdushnoy Oborony* (usually referred to as 'PVO'), operated as a separate entity, distinct from the VVS, controlling anti-aircraft artillery, surface-to-air missiles and interceptor aircraft in an integrated defence network of the entire Soviet Union, though after 1980 all their fighter aircraft were transferred to Air Force control. Naval aviation, including maritime patrol, anti-shipping and shipborne fixed-wing aircraft and helicopters were the domain of Soviet Naval Aviation (*Aviatsiya Voyenno-Morskogo Flota,* the 'AV-MF').

Technological zenith

In terms of size, the VVS was second only to the United States Air Force for most of the duration of the Cold War, though at its peak in the 1980s the Soviet Air Force was the world's largest with around 10,000 aircraft in operational service. At this point the service was arguably also at its technological zenith, with combat aircraft that delivered parity with contemporary Western types or were comfortably superior to them.

End of Soviet Union

The abrupt dissolution of the USSR in December 1991 saw this awesomely powerful force summarily carved up into the air arms of the various Soviet successor states; the largest, taking 40 per cent of then-operational Soviet aircraft, was the nascent Russian Air Force, which still operates many Cold War types, and which is, today, the World's second largest air force (the US Air Force still being the largest).

FIGHTERS

The USSR had long produced fighters that pushed contemporary technology to its limits. During the Cold War the MiG-15 and MiG-21 became the iconic Warsaw Pact fighters of their respective eras and during the 1970s and 80s the MiG-29 and Su-27 were arguably the best in the world. The Soviet Union also produced a swathe of less familiar fighter aircraft, all of which are described below.

- Yakovlev Yak-9 'Frank'
- Lavochkin La-9 'Fritz' and La-11 'Fang'
- Mikoyan-Gurevich MiG-9 'Fargo'
- Yakovlev Yak-15 and Yak-17 'Feather'
- Yakovlev Yak-23 'Flora'
- Lavochkin La-15 'Fantail'
- Mikoyan-Gurevich MiG-15 'Fagot'
- Mikoyan-Gurevich MiG-17 'Fresco'
- Mikoyan-Gurevich MiG-19 'Farmer'
- Yakovlev Yak-25 'Flashlight'
- Mikoyan-Gurevich MiG-21 'Fishbed'
- Sukhoi Su-9 and Su-11 'Fishpot'
- Tupolev Tu-128 'Fiddler'
- Sukhoi Su-15 'Flagon'
- Mikoyan-Gurevich MiG-25 'Foxbat'
- Mikoyan-Gurevich MiG-23 'Flogger'
- Yakovlev Yak-38 'Forger'
- Mikoyan-Gurevich MiG-31 'Foxhound'
- Sukhoi Su-27 'Flanker'
- Mikoyan MiG-29 'Fulcrum'

Fast, agile, tough, and very heavily armed, no other Soviet fighter aircraft caused as much consternation in the West as the remarkable MiG-15.

FIGHTERS

Yakovlev Yak-9 'Frank'

The Yakovlev Yak-9 was developed during World War II from the Yakovlev Yak-7, itself a variant of Yakovlev's original fighter design, the Yakovlev Yak-1. Following the cessation of hostilities, the Yak-9 enjoyed a lengthy period of postwar service and saw action again over Korea.

The Yak-9 derivative of the basic Yak fighter design first flew in October 1942 and had been continually developed throughout the war years. Proving highly successful, over 14,500 examples had been built by the end of hostilities, and the Yak-9 would remain an important element of the Soviet fighter force for the rest of the decade.

New metal structure

During 1945, the basic structure of the Yak fighter was in the process of changing from a wooden airframe covered in plywood and fabric skinning to a predominately metal structure. The Yak-9U was just beginning to enter service and also introduced a more powerful Klimov M-107A engine, which delivered high performance, though at the expense of reliability, and early batches of the Yak-9U featured the M-105 PF-3 engine.

Postwar development resulted in the definitive piston-engined Yak fighter, the Yak-9P. This fighter appeared in 1946, by which time light alloy supply was sufficiently assured to allow for the aircraft to be fitted with an all-metal wing for the first time. This meant it was easily distinguished from earlier variants by its elliptical wingtips, which were both stronger and more durable than its mixed construction forebears.

The Yak-9P retained the delightful handling for which the Yak series of fighters were famed but combined this with a greater fuel capacity and more reliable VK-107 engine, producing a useful improvement over the preceding Yak-9U.

Korean War action

In production until December 1948, Yak-9Ps were used in large numbers by Soviet forces, as well as being widely exported to several Warsaw Pact nations. The aircraft was one of the first Soviet fighter types to be encountered in the Korean War, clashing on several occasions with US North American P-51Ds and Vought F4U-4 Corsairs – which shared a broadly similar performance to the Yakovlev fighter – and in 1950, at least one F-80C Shooting Star jet fell to the guns of a North Korean Yak-9P.

Yak-9P

North Korea had received at least 79 Yak-9s by 1950 and this example was captured intact and airworthy at Kimpo Airfield on 17 September that year. Though it was shipped to the US and evaluated there, it was scrapped in 1958.

Yakovlev Yak-9P

Weight (maximum take-off): 3820kg (8422lb)
Dimensions: Length 8.5m (27ft 11in), Wingspan 9.74m (32ft), Height 3m (9ft 10in)
Powerplant: One 1119kW (1500hp) Klimov VK-107A V12 liquid-cooled piston engine
Maximum speed: 690km/h (430mph)
Range: 1130km (702 miles)
Ceiling: 10,500m (34,450ft)
Crew: 1
Armament: One 20mm (0.8in) ShVAK cannon and one 12.7mm (0.5in) Berezin UBS machine gun fixed forward firing in forward fuselage decking

Lavochkin La-9 'Fritz' and La-11 'Fang'

The culmination of a family of highly successful radial-engined fighter aircraft from Lavochkin, the postwar Lavochkin La-9 and near-identical La-11 formed an important part of the Soviet fighter force in the immediate postwar years.

Bearing a superficial resemblance to Lavochkin's highly successful La-7, flown by many successful pilots, including the Allied ace-of-aces, Ivan Kozhedub, the La-9 was, in fact, a new design, featuring all-metal construction throughout as opposed to the mixed wood and metal airframe of the earlier machine.

New type

Despite using the same ASh-82FN engine as its predecessor, the new aircraft was around 30kmh (20mph) faster and considerably longer-ranged, and it was ordered into production following a successful first flight on 16 June 1946.

Early in its service life, a need was discovered for a longer-ranged variant, and this was answered by the externally near-indistinguishable La-11. This variant featured more fuel tanks and reduced the armament to three cannon as opposed to the La-9's four, but in all other respects, it was essentially identical. Both demonstrated outstanding performance at low and medium altitudes.

Production and service

The Lavochkins were built in large numbers – 1559 of the La-9 and 1232 of the La-11 – and both were exported to China and North Korea. In China, La-11s remained in service as late as 1966.

In the tense international situation during the early years of the Cold War, Lavochkin fighters were involved in several combat incidents: in 1950, Soviet La-11s shot down a US Navy PB4Y-2 Privateer operating in the intelligence role over the Baltic along with a USN P2V Neptune later in the year. More infamous was the downing of a civilian Cathay Pacific C-54 airliner by a pair of Chinese La-11s in 1954.

Both Lavochkin types saw significant service during the Korean War, and it was the comparatively poor altitude performance of the type when attempting to intercept the B-29 Superfortress that proved the direct impetus for sending MiG-15s to Korea.

La-11

Well armed and fast, the La-11 was much the same size as the contemporary Grumman F8F Bearcat but was around two tonnes lighter when loaded. Like the wartime La-7, both La-9 and La-11 were noted for their outstanding handling.

Lavochkin La-11

Weight (maximum take-off): 3996kg (8810lb)
Dimensions: Length 8.62m (28ft 3in), Wingspan 9.8m (32ft 2in), Height 3.47m (11ft 5in)
Powerplant: One 1380 kW (1850 hp) Shvetsov ASh-82FN 14-cylinder air-cooled radial piston engine
Maximum speed: 674km/h (419mph)
Range: 2235km (1389 miles)
Ceiling: 10,250m (33,630ft)
Crew: 1
Armament: Three 23mm (0.91in) Nudelman-Suranov NS-23 cannon fixed forward firing in forward fuselage decking

FIGHTERS

Mikoyan-Gurevich MiG-9 'Fargo'

The Soviet Union's first jet fighter to fly (but only just), the Mikoyan-Gurevich MiG-9 was a conservative design but proved the best of the Soviet Union's first jet fighter designs and paved the way for the future dominance of the MiG design bureau.

Designed around a pair of reverse-engineered BMW 003 turbojets, work on the MiG-9 began early in 1945. Adopting a pod and boom configuration with a tricycle undercarriage (the first such installation fitted to a Soviet-designed fighter) allowed for the engines to be placed close together under the forward fuselage, minimizing asymmetric thrust issues in the event of engine failure, a likely occurrence given the low standard of reliability offered by the 003 engines.

First Soviet jet aircraft

In all other respects, however, the MiG-9 was a low-risk conventional design with its unswept wing and non-pressurized cockpit. Following taxi tests, the MiG-9 became the first Soviet jet aircraft to fly on 24 April 1946, two hours before the first flight of the Yak-15, the honour of making the first Soviet jet flight being decided by the toss of a coin.

The first 10 aircraft were powered by refurbished 003 engines, as the reverse-engineered Soviet-built copy (designated the RD-20) was not yet available. They were built in great haste with the intention of being flown in the 7 November Tushino Air Parade. So much effort was expended on this endeavour that serial production aircraft were delayed. Production MiG-9s proved simple to fly and as such served as a good introduction for Soviet fighter pilots to transition to jet propulsion.

Flaming engines

The aircraft was gradually improved over its production life, with cockpit pressurization, an ejection seat and airbrakes added to later batches and retrofitted to early production machines. One problem that was never entirely solved despite numerous modifications was the armament: firing the 37mm (1.46in) cannon tended to result in the engines flaming out after a few rounds. Despite this impediment, the MiG-9 was clearly superior to contemporary rival Yakovlev fighters and placed the MiG design bureau firmly into a position of ascendency that it would largely maintain for the next 40 years.

MiG-9

The MiG-9 was very well armed, though firing all three guns resulted in regular engine flameouts, a problem that was never entirely solved. The long barrels of the single 37mm (1.46in) and two 23mm (0.91in) guns were mistaken for pitot tubes by Western observers.

Mikoyan-Gurevich MiG-9

Weight (maximum take-off): 4860kg (10,714lb)
Dimensions: Length 9.75m (32ft), Wingspan 10m (32ft 10in), Height 3.23m (10ft 7in)
Powerplant: Two RD-20 turbojet engines, each rated at 7.80kN (1,754lbf) thrust
Maximum speed: 910km/h (570mph)
Range: 800km (500 miles)
Ceiling: 13,000m (43,000ft)
Crew: 1
Armament: One 37mm (1.46in) Nudelman N-37 cannon fixed forward firing in nose intake divider and two 23mm (0.91in) Nudelman-Suranov NS-23 cannon fixed, forward firing in underside of nose intake

Yakovlev Yak-15 and Yak-17 'Feather'

Despite appearing triumphantly in the May Day Flypast in 1947 and being much publicized in postwar propaganda, the early Yakovlev jets were extremely limited in capability but boasted excellent handling and enjoyed some success in the training role.

One of only two piston engine fighters adapted for jet power to enter production (the other being the SAAB J-21), the Yakovlev Yak-15 consisted of a Yak-3 airframe with a reverse-engineered Junkers Jumo 004 turbojet mounted in place of the V-12 piston engine in the nose and exhausting under the centre section.

Flown for the first time on 24 April 1946, the Yak-15 was not a particularly successful fighter; its tailwheel undercarriage led to the jet engine exhaust, damaging airfields and taxiways, and fuel and oil would often drip onto the engine, leading to a cockpit filled with arid smoke. Top speed was low, and the aircraft's range was woefully short, but the Yak-15 demonstrated excellent handling characteristics inherited from the Yak-3 and was easy to fly. As a result, the Yak-15 served as an excellent conversion trainer for introducing Soviet fighter pilots to jet propulsion.

Yak-17

The urgent requirement for a tricycle undercarriage led to the Yak-17, featuring a small nosewheel that retracted into a fairing below the engine. The relocation of the main gear rearward in the wing took up space previously used for fuel tanks, and as a result, the Yak-17 featured a pair of 200l (44 gal) drop tanks mounted under the wingtips. Although a few single-seat Yak-17s were built, the aircraft inherited the poor performance and range of its Yak-15 forebear as well as its simple flying characteristics, enhanced by the simpler ground handling of the tricycle undercarriage.

Most of the approximate total of 430 Yak-17s built were of the Yak-17UTI two-seat training variant, assigned the reporting name 'Magnet' by NATO. A few Yak-17UTIs were exported to other Warsaw Pact nations, but all had been withdrawn from service by the early 1960s.

Yak-17

Switching from taildragger to tricycle undercarriage resulted in a huge improvement to the ground handling of the Yak fighter. The mounting of the nosewheel in its external fairing under the engine however belies the somewhat extemporised nature of this modification.

Yakovlev Yak-17

Weight (maximum take-off): 3323kg (7326lb)
Dimensions: Length 8.78m (28ft 10in), Wingspan 9.2m (30ft 2in), Height 2.3m (7ft 7in)
Powerplant: One Klimov RD-10A turbojet engine rated at 9.8kN (2,200lbf) thrust
Maximum speed: 744km/h (462mph)
Range: 395km (245 miles)
Ceiling: 11,900m (39,000ft)
Crew: 1
Armament: Two 23mm (0.91in) Nudelman-Suranov NS-23K cannon fixed, forward firing above nose intake

FIGHTERS

Yakovlev Yak-23 'Flora'

Although it persisted with the outmoded nose-mounted engine configuration of the Yak-15 and 17, the Yakovlev Yak-23 was an altogether more formidable machine with an impressive rate of climb.

In March 1947, Yakovlev, along with several other design bureau, were ordered to develop a single-seat fighter to be powered by the British Rolls-Royce Nene engine. The resultant Yak-23 resembled the Yak-17 in general layout but was an all-new design featuring a semi-monocoque fuselage mated to an unswept laminar flow wing.

Unlike the earlier aircraft, the tricycle undercarriage could now be retracted fully into the fuselage and a greater fuel load was carried internally that could also be augmented with a 195l (43 gal) drop tank mounted under each wingtip. Work on the prototype was swift, and the type made its first flight on 8 July 1947, appearing in public during a flypast at Tushino airbase in August of the same year.

Mixed package

Although praised for its handling as well as its excellent acceleration and climb performance, the Yak-23 was criticized for its unpressurized cockpit, weak armament and heavy controls. Most of these issues were ameliorated or eradicated in the second prototype, though the armament remained unchanged, and the Yak-23 was approved for production.

Brief service

Soviet service was brief – after entering the air arm in late 1949, the obvious superiority of the superlative MiG-15 saw the Yaks withdrawn in 1951. Ultimately, 316 production aircraft would be built, over half of which would be built for export.

Major customers for the Yak-23 included Czechoslovakia, Romania and the largest export customer, Poland, which took delivery of 100 of the type. In Polish service, the aircraft would achieve a brief moment of fame when, in September 1957, pilot Andrzej Abłamowicz set two world records in the Yak-23 by climbing to 3000m (9843ft) in 119 seconds and 6000m (19,685ft) in 197 seconds.

Yak-23

This is the third prototype Yak-23 fitted with the optional underwing tip tanks. Soviet use of the Yak-23 did not last long, production of the aircraft having been authorised only due to delays to the MiG-15 and La-15 programmes.

Yakovlev Yak-23

Weight (maximum take-off): 3384kg (7460lb)
Dimensions: Length 8.13m (26ft 8in), Wingspan 8.73m (28ft 8in), Height 3.31m (10ft 10in)
Powerplant: One Klimov RD-500 centrifugal-flow turbojet engine rated at 15.6kN (3,500lbf)
Maximum speed: 925km/h (575mph)
Range: 1200km (750 miles)
Ceiling: 14,800m (48,600ft)
Crew: 1
Armament: Two 23mm (0.91in) Nudelman-Rikhter NR-23 (0.91in) cannon fixed, forward firing above nose intake

LAVOCHKIN LA-15 'FANTAIL'

The Mikoyan-Gurevich MiG-15's initial rival, Lavochkin's La-15, was superior in some respects to the vaunted MiG fighter but was built in trivial numbers and saw only brief operational service.

The last Lavochkin fighter to enter production, the La-15 owed its existence to Lavochkin's pioneering work in the field of swept wings, the design bureau having built the first Soviet swept wing aircraft: the La-160. Although boasting a highly advanced wing (believed to be the thinnest in the world when it first flew), the La-160 featured an ungainly fuselage, with the engine mounted ahead of the cockpit as with contemporary Yakovlev fighters. Lavochkin followed this up with a Rolls-Royce Nene-powered fighter prototype, the La-168, with the engine moved to the rear fuselage.

A backup aircraft of the same basic design but scaled down by 10 per cent with a lower-powered Rolls-Royce Derwent was also produced and named 'Aircraft 174'. This proved only 6 per cent slower than the Nene-powered aircraft and demonstrated excellent handling and agility, so, with several other Soviet programmes requiring the use of the Nene, the decision was made to put Aircraft 174 into production as the La-15.

Entering service in early 1949, the lightweight La-15 proved very popular with its pilots on account of its excellent flying qualities, and although it couldn't match the MiG-15 for outright performance, the La-15 was more manoeuvrable and easier to fly. Unfortunately for Lavochkin, the MiG-15 possessed a better rate of climb, essential for the interception role that the Soviet authorities saw as the main purpose of the new jet fighters. Perhaps even more crucially, the MiG was also simpler and cheaper to build. As a result, only 235 La-15s were built (as opposed to over 17,000 MiG-15s), and all were withdrawn in 1953.

The sole surviving La-15 is preserved at the Central Air Force Museum in Monino, east of Moscow.

Lavochkin La-15 'Fantail'
Weight (maximum take-off): 3850kg (8488lb)
Dimensions: Length 9.56m (31ft 5in), Wingspan 8.83m (29ft), Height 3.8m (12ft 5in)
Powerplant: One Klimov RD-500 centrifugal-flow turbojet engine rated at 15.59kN (3500lbf)
Maximum speed: 1007km/h (626mph)
Range: 1145km (711 miles)
Ceiling: 13500m (44300ft)
Crew: 1
Armament: Three 23mm (0.91in) Nudelman-Suranov NS-23 cannon fixed, forward firing

---

Yak-23

The Yak-23 enjoyed a longer period of service with other Warsaw Pact air forces and the type was held in high regard by Polish pilots for its excellent handling. This colourful example was on the strength of the Polish Air Force in 1955.

FIGHTERS

Mikoyan-Gurevich MiG-15 'Fagot'

A highly influential aircraft, the Mikoyan-Gurevich MiG-15 remains the world's most produced jet aircraft. Following dazzling combat use in the Korean War, the MiG-15 saw service with dozens of nations and operated for many years as an advanced trainer.

Designed around Soviet-manufactured unlicensed copies of the Rolls-Royce Nene engine, the RD-45 and later VK-1, the MiG-15 placed Soviet aircraft firmly at the forefront of international fighter design as the British-designed engines reliably delivered much greater thrust than had previously been available to Soviet designers.

Also crucial to the MiG-15's success was its swept wing, which benefited from captured Focke-Wulf plans and wind-tunnel models towards the end of the war. The extent to which the MiG-15 derived from these plans is still debated today, but the aircraft does bear a similarity in overall design to the Focke-Wulf Ta 183, the prototype of which was under construction at the end of hostilities, particularly its mid-mounted wing swept at 35 degrees with slight anhedral. Unlike the Ta 183, however, the MiG featured the horizontal tail surfaces mounted halfway down the highly swept vertical tail surface rather than atop it and utilized prominent wing fences to prevent spanwise airflow, which can result in portions of swept wings becoming stalled if left unchecked.

Advanced wing

The MiG-15's advanced wing was first flown on a piston-engined canard aircraft, the MiG-8 *Utka* (Duck), in 1945, before the construction of the first prototype of the new fighter, then designated I-310. Intended primarily to destroy heavy bombers, such as the B-29, the I-310 featured the potent armament of two Nudelman-Suranov NS-23 23mm (0.91in) cannon on the left-hand side of the fuselage as well as a single 37mm (1.46in) Nudelman weapon on the right.

From the outset, the cannons and ammunition were housed in a quickly detachable pack in the lower forward fuselage, and in service, a fresh set of guns and ammunition could be readied for the aircraft on the ground, allowing for high-speed re-arming. The I-310

MiG-15bis

One of the VVS MiG-15s stationed in China in 1951, '384 White' was reportedly flown by 19-kill ace Yevgeny Pepelyayev during the Korean War. 14 of Pepelyayev's victories were over the MiG-15's great rival, the F-86 Sabre.

Mikoyan-Gurevich MiG-15bis

Weight (maximum take-off): 6106kg (13,461lb)
Dimensions: Length 10.1m (33ft 2in), Wingspan 10.09m (33ft 1in), Height 3.7m (12ft 2in)
Powerplant: One Klimov VK-1 centrifugal-flow turbojet engine rated at 26.5kN (5,950lbf)
Maximum speed: 1076km/h (669mph)
Range (with drop tanks): 1200km (746 miles)
Ceiling: 15,500m (50,900ft)
Crew: 1
Armament: Two 23mm (0.91) Nudelman-Rikhter NR-23 cannon in the lower left fuselage and one 37mm (1.46in) Nudelman N-37 cannon in the lower right fuselage; up to 500kg (1100lb) bombs or unguided rockets

flew for the first time on 30 December 1947, two months after the first XP-86 Sabre, which also featured a wing derived from late-war German research and which would become the MiG-15's primary opponent.

Exceptional performance

Immediately demonstrating excellent performance, the I-310 was selected for mass production as the MiG-15, the first production example flying almost exactly a year after the first prototype on 31 December 1948. Six months later, the aircraft was revealed to the public at the Tushino Air Parade when a single example was displayed, but ever-increasing numbers were quickly made available, such that by the 1950 May Day air show, no fewer than 139 MiG-15s took part.

From the start, the MiG-15's performance was exceptional, particularly in rate of climb and top speed, though early aircraft were susceptible to rolling left or right due to manufacturing inconsistencies, a problem solved by the addition of simple ground-adjustable trim tabs called *nozhi* (knives). Introduced into service over the course of 1949, the new MiG proved popular with pilots due to its generally easy handling characteristics and comfortable cockpit with excellent air conditioning and heating. Ground crews also appreciated the aircraft, which was simple and easy to maintain.

Less impressive initially was the MiG-15's range, and modifications to improve this aspect of the aircraft's performance took place almost immediately after the MiG entered production, with provision to carry a pair of external fuel tanks, initially of 250L (55 gal) capacity but soon increased to 300L (66 gal), 400L (88 gal) and finally 600L (132 gal).

MiG-15bis

Aircraft with the provision to carry external tanks were soon followed by the more comprehensively improved MiG-15bis, featuring the more powerful VK-1 engine; a pair of Nudelman-Richter NR-23 cannon replacing the slower firing NS-23s; the OSP-48 instrument landing system; larger airbrakes; and a revised canopy with improve visibility; which flew for the first time in September 1949. By the time production switched to the MiG-15bis during 1950, 1344 MiG-15s had been built in the USSR, and these would be followed by 8352 single-seat examples of the MiG-15bis.

First combat

1950 saw the MiG-15 committed to combat. Despite its famous use in the Korean War, the MiG-15 actually made its combat debut in the Chinese Civil War after Mao Zedong requested assistance from the Soviet Union. Soviet pilots transferred with MiG-15s to introduce Chinese pilots to the new jet fighter as well as undertake combat sorties themselves. The MiG-15 scored its first victory on 28 April 1950, when a Nationalist Chinese P-38 Lightning was shot down, followed up on 11 May by the destruction of a B-24 Liberator.

Mikoyan-Gurevich MiG-15UTI

Weight (maximum take-off): 6045kg (13,327lb)
Dimensions: Length 10.10m (33ft, 2in), Wingspan 10.08m (33ft, 1in), Height 3.7m (12ft, 2in)
Powerplant: One Klimov VK-1 centrifugal-flow turbojet engine rated at 26.5kN (5,950lbf)
Maximum speed: 1050km/h (652mph)
Range (with drop tanks): 1860km (1156 miles)
Ceiling: 15,500m (50,853ft)
Crew: 2
Armament: None

MiG-15UTI

Pictured as it appeared during the mid-1950s, '28 Blue' was one of the countless MiG-15 trainers operated by the Soviet Union for nearly the entire Cold War.

FIGHTERS

On 26 June 1950, the Korean War broke out, and the inability of the Yak-9Ps of the North Korean Air Force to successfully intercept the high-flying B-29s prompted requests for Soviet assistance. The Kremlin agreed to supply MiG-15s to both the North Koreans and Chinese, as well as transfer many Soviet aircrew to the theatre to fly combat missions themselves, though at the time this was denied.

Flying against the Boeing B-29 Superfortress, the specific aircraft that the MiG had been designed to destroy, the MiG-15s proved highly successful. For example, on 12 April 1951, MiG-15s shot down or damaged beyond repair 10 B-29As, as well as four escort fighters, for the loss of only one of their own. By the end of 1951, B-29 losses to MiG-15s were severe enough to prompt Far East Air Forces High Command to cancel daylight attacks by B-29s and only undertake night raids.

Head-to-head

The appearance of the new swept-wing fighter over Korea caused a sensation, as it quickly demonstrated its superiority over all Western types currently in the theatre, prompting the rushed deployment of three squadrons of the F-86 Sabre, America's only operational swept-wing fighter, to Korea in December. The MiG-15 and F-86 were very closely matched, with the MiG-15 demonstrating somewhat superior high-altitude performance, though at lower altitudes, the F-86 maintained a slight advantage. The MiG's cannon armament possessed more destructive power than the six machine guns of the Sabre, but this was offset somewhat by the cannon's relatively slow rate of fire and the different ballistic trajectories of the 23mm (0.9in) and 37mm (1.46in) weapons, making aiming difficult.

Robust airframe

The MiG had a very robust airframe that proved difficult to seriously damage by machine gun fire alone. Probably the greatest flaw of the MiG, however, was its problematic handling quirks at the top end of its performance envelope. The F-86 could be dived beyond the speed of sound, yet the MiG-15 was limited to Mach 0.92, and the MiG also possessed a propensity to stall without warning and enter a spin that was nearly impossible to recover from.

There were 56 recorded instances of UN pilots witnessing a MiG-15 entering a spin in combat, at least 25 of which resulted in crashes. Despite these impediments, however, the MiG-15 established an enviable combat record over Korea, and at least 16 Soviet pilots became aces with five victories or more, as well as several Chinese and North Koreans. The top scorer in Korea was Major Nikolay Sutyagin, credited with 22 victories.

MiG-15UTI

All the Warsaw Pact nations made use of the MiG-15, particularly the trainer variants. This example served with the Czechoslovakian Air Force and is now preserved at the Kbely Aviation Museum near Prague.

Mikoyan-Gurevich MiG-15UTI

Weight (maximum take-off): 6045kg (13,327lb)
Dimensions: Length 10.10m (33ft, 2in), Wingspan 10.08m (33ft, 1in), Height 3.7m (12ft, 2in)
Powerplant: One Klimov VK-1 centrifugal-flow turbojet engine rated at 26.5kN (5,950lbf)
Maximum speed: 1050km/h (652mph)
Range (with drop tanks): 1860km (1156 miles)
Ceiling: 15,500m (50,853ft)
Crew: 2
Armament: None

FIGHTERS

Lim-1

Licence production of the basic MiG-15 single seater was undertaken at the WSK-Mielec factory in Poland as the Lim-1. 227 Lim-1s were built, including this one, along with 500 examples of the MiG-15bis as the Lim-2.

As well as its Soviet production, the single-seat MiG-15 was built under licence by Poland as the Lim-1 and -2, and in Czechoslovakia as the S-102 and S-103, and as early as 1949, a two-seat training version, the MiG-15UTI, had been flown. As a training aircraft, assigned the NATO reporting name 'Midget', the MiG-15 would enjoy an incredible longevity of service, still being utilized by the North Korean People's Air Force in 2019, some 70 years after its first flight.

Increasing numbers of MiG-15s, particularly the two-seater variants, are now flying in civilian hands – 43 examples were on the US civil register in 2011. Many of the two-seaters were converted from earlier Soviet and Czech single-seaters in Poland as the SBLim-1 and -2, and China also produced an unknown amount of two-seat MiG-15s as the JJ-2. As a result, exact production figures for the MiG-15 are unknown, but over 17,000 are known to have been built.

Lim-1

Weight (maximum take-off): 6105kg (13,458lb)
Dimensions: Length 10.1m (33ft 2in), Wingspan 10.09m (33ft 1in), Height 3.7m (12ft 2in)
Powerplant: One Lis-1 (licence built Klimov VK-1) centrifugal-flow turbojet engine rated at 26.5kN (5,950lbf) thrust
Maximum speed: 1076km/h (669mph)
Range: 1200km (746 miles)
Ceiling: 15,500m (50,900ft)
Crew: 1
Armament: Two 23mm (0.91) Nudelman-Rikhter NR-23 cannon in the lower left fuselage and one 37mm (1.46in) Nudelman N-37 cannon in the lower right fuselage; up to 500kg (1100lb) bombs or unguided rockets

The MiG-15 in two-seat form became near-ubiquitous as an advanced trainer and virtually every Warsaw Pact fighter pilot trained on the type. Yuri Gagarin, the first human in space, lost his life in a MiG-15UTI crash during a routine flight, the cause of which remains unclear.

FIGHTERS

Mikoyan-Gurevich MiG-17 'Fresco'

Derived from the Mikoyan-Gurevich MiG-15, which it closely resembled, the Mikoyan-Gurevich MiG-17 offered a useful increase in performance while eliminating the worst flaws of the earlier aircraft. It remained competitive against faster, more modern aircraft well into the 1960s.

As early as 1949, the MiG design bureau was working on a significantly reworked derivative of the MiG-15 that was then entering service. The primary change to the earlier aircraft was its wing, which was both thinner and more highly swept, 45 degrees at the root and 42 degrees towards the wingtip. Despite its slimmer profile, the new wing was also stiffer than that of the MiG-15 and could better resist twisting and bending at high speeds. The wing could be easily identified as it now featured a third fence on either side. The fuselage was slightly longer than the MiG-15, gun armament remained unchanged, and although it utilized the same VK-1 engine as its predecessor, the new aircraft's maximum speed was increased by 40–50km/h (25–31mph), and the fighter possessed better manoeuvrability at high altitude. Flown for the first time as the I-330 'SI' in January 1951, the aircraft was authorized for production in September 1951 and designated the MiG-17, reflecting the significant changes that had been made to the airframe.

Quantity production was initially delayed in favour of producing as many MiG-15s as possible, which were urgently required for the Korean conflict. As a result, no MiG-17s saw service during the Korean War. Production MiG-17s featured the ASP-4N gunsight and SRC-3 gun ranging radar, which were a copy of the optical gunsight and SRD-3 gun ranging radar taken from a captured F-86 Sabre. Initial deliveries of the basic MiG-17 were followed by 225 examples of an all-weather interceptor variant with the Izumrud RP-1 radar designated the MiG-17P. Further development of the basic fighter resulted in the more potent MiG-17F, which utilized the VK-1F afterburning engine with a new convergent-divergent jet nozzle and updated fuel system.

Initially, the alloys used in the nozzle body and stator vanes were insufficiently heat resistant to allow the afterburner to be used for extended periods, so early MiG-17Fs utilized a separate tank to supply fuel to the afterburner with a 90 per cent ethanol content due to its lower temperature combustion. Later production aircraft benefited from improved metallurgy and used normal fuel. The afterburning engine transformed the MiG-17's performance, doubling the rate of climb and greatly improving vertical

MiG-17

Serving with the VVS during August 1968, this MiG-17 is pictured as it appeared during the invasion of Czechoslovakia.

Mikoyan-Gurevich MiG-17 'Fresco'
Weight (maximum take-off): 5930kg (13,073lb)
Dimensions: Length 11.26m (36ft 11in), Wingspan 9.6m (31ft 6in), Height 3.8m (12ft 6in)
Powerplant: One Klimov VK-1A centrifugal flow turbojet engine rated at 26.48kN (5953lbf)
Maximum speed: 1114km/h (692mph)
Range: 1295km (805 miles)
Ceiling: 15,600m (51,181ft)
Crew: 1
Armament: Two 23mm (0.91) Nudelman-Rikhter NR-23 cannon in the lower left fuselage and one 37mm (1.46in) Nudelman N-37 cannon in the lower right fuselage; up to 500kg (1100lb) bombs or unguided rockets

FIGHTERS

manoeuvres. It also allowed the aircraft to briefly attain supersonic speed in a shallow dive, although the aircraft would regularly suffer from an uncommanded pitch-up just below Mach 1. Again, the MiG-17F was also built in all-weather form with the Izumrud RP-2 air interception radar mounted in a bullet fairing in the upper section of the nose intake and designated the MiG-17PF. Like the MiG-15 before it, the MiG-17 was licence-produced in Poland as the Lim-5 and the Lim-5P all-weather variant. Poland also developed a dedicated strike variant, the Lim-5M and improved Lim-6bis, which would remain Poland's most numerous strike aircraft until the mid-1980s. China also built the aircraft as the Shenyang J-5 and a dedicated export variant designated the F-5.

First combat

Combat use of the MiG-17 was limited in Soviet hands as the aircraft was quickly superseded by true supersonic interceptors, such as the MiG-19 and MiG-21, although four MiG-17s shot down a C-130 Hercules over Armenia that was likely engaged in covert reconnaissance. The vast majority of active service use of the MiG-17 took place with the air arms of other nations, not least due to the MiG-17's considerable success on the export market: the aircraft would serve with every Warsaw Pact nation and over 25 other nations worldwide.

In North Vietnamese hands in particular, the MiG-17 gained considerable notoriety for its ability to successfully combat more sophisticated American aircraft during the Vietnam War, despite its subsonic performance and relatively elderly design. The MiG-17 was the first jet fighter to be operated by the North Vietnamese, and the first victories came when two Mach-2 capable F-105 Thunderchiefs were downed on 4 April 1965, although three MiG-17s were also lost. Vietnamese pilots found that their nimble MiG-17s could outmanoeuvre the larger and heavier US aircraft, and the cannon armament proved effective. Even if no US aircraft were destroyed, the MiG-17 attacks, usually mounted in concert with the faster MiG-21, would succeed in forcing the fighter bombers to jettison their bombs without attacking their assigned target. In total, 71 aircraft were claimed by VPAF pilots from 1965 to 1972, of which 28 aircraft were admitted lost to the MiGs by the US, including 11 F-4 Phantoms and eight F-105 Thunderchiefs. The success of the

Lim-6bis
The additional inboard underwing pylons and bullet fairing for a braking parachute indicate that this is a Polish manufactured Lim-6bis close support variant. As well as Poland, the Lim-6bis was operated by East Germany, Egypt, and Indonesia.

Lim-6bis
Weight (maximum take-off): 6652kg (14,665lb)
Dimensions: Length 11.36m (37ft 3in), Wingspan 9.63m (31ft 7in), Height: 3.8m (12ft 6in)
Powerplant: One Lis-5 (licence built Klimov VK-1F) centrifugal-flow turbojet engine rated at 33.1kN (7,400lbf)
Maximum speed: 1150km/h (710mph)
Range: 1080km (670 miles)
Ceiling: 16,470m (54,040ft)
Crew: 1
Armament: Two 23mm (0.91) Nudelman-Rikhter NR-23 cannon in the lower left fuselage and one 37mm (1.46in) Nudelman N-37 cannon in the lower right fuselage; up to 780kg (1720lb) of bombs, rocket launchers or stores

---

light and nimble aircraft resulted in the USAF initiating project 'Feather Duster' to develop tactics that allowed heavier American fighters to deal with small and agile opponents like the MiG-17. To simulate the MiG-17 in training missions, the USAF utilized the F-86H Sabre. However, in 1968, the US managed to obtain the first of two ex-Syrian MiG-17s

FIGHTERS

for evaluation, and this was also used covertly for combat training selected USAF and USN aircrew.

Middle Eastern wars

Further combat use occurred in the Middle East. Egypt had been an early customer for the MiG-17, receiving their first aircraft in 1956, and although Egypt had largely avoided using their MiG-17s during the Suez crisis, Egyptian MiG-17s were later committed to the North Yemen Civil War and again during the Six Day War, along with similar aircraft operated by Syria, Jordan and Iraq.

Egyptian MiG-17s were utilized again as late as 1973 during the Yom Kippur War but were retired from frontline use shortly afterwards. Other nations to operate the MiG-17 in combat were Nigeria during the Nigerian Civil War and Sri Lanka during the 1971 insurgency in that country.

Like the MiG-15 before it, the MiG-17 was developed into a two-seat trainer, the MiG-17UTI, also produced in China as the Shenyang JJ-5, which would remain in service for decades after the single-seat version had been retired. China retired its remaining JJ-5s in 1992, though 200 Shenyang-built two-seaters were still in service with North Korea in 2021. Several MiG-17s have also made their way into civilian hands, with 17 examples, mostly Polish-built, recorded on the US civil register in 2022.

MiG-17PF

The 'beak' above the intake and the radome visible within it contained the Izumrud radar of the MiG-17PF all-weather fighter. East Germany operated the MiG-17PF variant from 1959 to 1973.

MiG-17F

Wearing the Romanian roundel markings re-adopted in 1984, this MiG-17F was one of a few dozen supplied to the nation in the mid fifties. This aircraft was photographed, in derelict condition, at Craiova Airbase in 1996.

Mikoyan-Gurevich MiG-17F

Weight (maximum take-off): 6069kg (13,380lb)
Dimensions: 11.26m (36ft 11in), Wingspan 9.63m (31ft 7in), Height 3.8m (12ft 6in)
Powerplant: One Klimov VK-1F centrifugal-flow turbojet engine rated at 26.5kN (6,000lbf) dry, 33.8kN (7,600lbf) with afterburner
Maximum speed: 1145km/h (711mph)
Range: 2020km (1260 miles)
Ceiling: 16,600m (54,500ft)
Crew: 1
Armament: Two 23mm (0.91in) Nudelman-Rikhter NR-23 cannon and one 37 mm (1.46in) Nudelman N-37 cannon fixed, forward firing under nose intake; up to 500kg bomb, rocket launchers or stores

Mikoyan-Gurevich MiG-19 'Farmer'

The Soviet Union's first supersonic production aircraft, the Mikoyan-Gurevich MiG-19 was a significant milestone in Soviet fighter design. Like the MiG-17 before it, the MiG-19 saw its most intense combat service in the skies over North Vietnam.

Work on what was to become the MiG-19 began in 1950 to produce an aircraft with a better range than the MiG-17 and one that would be capable of exceeding Mach 1 in level flight. MiG built the I-340 and similar I-360 in 1951 and 1952 respectively, based on the MiG-17F but with two Mikulin AM-5 axial-flow turbojets mounted side-by-side in a new rear fuselage. This was then developed further into a completely new aircraft, becoming the first true prototype of the MiG-19 ('Farmer-A').

Initially flying on 5 January 1954, the aircraft demonstrated excellent performance and was ordered into mass production the following month, well before the conclusion of its official trials. Production aircraft featured a trio of 23mm (0.9in) NR-23 cannon and were fitted with two underwing pylons for bombs or drop tanks and a pair of removable pylons for unguided rockets aft of the main wheel wells. Deliveries to VVS units began in June 1955, and the aircraft was publicly revealed in July when 48 examples of the new fighter were displayed at the Tushino air show.

Teething problems

Unfortunately, the urgency attached to getting the aircraft into service had seen development rushed and early production aircraft experienced several in-flight explosions, caused by poor insulation between the aircraft's engines and the fuel tanks in the rear fuselage. The MiG-19 also displayed poor elevator control at supersonic speed, leading to the introduction of all-moving 'slab' horizontal tail surfaces on the improved MiG-19S (Farmer-C). Equipped with the *Svod* ('Vault') long-range navigation receiver, the MiG-19S had its gun armament upgraded to three 30mm (1.18in) NR-30 cannon, as well as providing for provisions for an ORO-32K unguided rocket pack or an FAB-250 bomb to be carried under each wing.

The MiG-19S entered production in 1956, by which time the MiG-19P (Farmer-B) all-weather fighter was also rolling off the production line. The MiG-19P had been developed in parallel to the regular day fighter and featured an RP-1 *Izumrud* ('Emerald') radar occupying two radomes in the

MiG-19S

The MiG-19S was the second major production variant of the 'Farmer' and introduced a swathe of improvements after early MiG-19s proved somewhat accident prone.

Mikoyan-Gurevich MiG-19S

Weight (maximum take-off): 8832kg (19,471lb)
Dimensions: Length 12.54m (41ft 2in), Wingspan 9m (29ft 6in), Height 3.88m (12ft 9in)
Powerplant: Two Tumansky RD-9B afterburning turbojet engines, each rated at 25.5kN (5700lbf) dry, 31.8kN (7,100lbf) with afterburner
Maximum speed: 1452km/h (902mph)
Range: 1390km (860 miles)
Ceiling: 17,500m (57,400ft)
Crew: 1
Armament: Three 30mm (1.18in) Nudelman-Rikhter NR-30 cannon, two fixed, forward firing in wing roots, one in lower forward fuselage; up to 500kg of stores

nose of the aircraft, one in a bullet fairing in the centre of the intake and the second on the top lip of the intake. With the radar utilizing space that was normally used by one of the cannon, gun armament was reduced to the two wing-mounted weapons, initially 23mm (0.9in) and later 30mm (1.18in). Later in the aircraft's service life, provision was added for the carriage of two Vympel K-13 missiles.

Further development in the USSR primarily focussed on improving the aircraft's altitude performance following the introduction of high-altitude reconnaissance balloons by the US as well as overflights of Soviet territory by RAF Canberra aircraft and later USAF U-2s, which were proving immune to interception by Soviet fighters. The lightened MiG-19SV, which was produced in small numbers, was developed to meet this threat with a lightened airframe, more powerful engines, and flaps arranged to give maximum lift at high altitudes.

The changes boosted the aircraft's ceiling by around 1000m (3000ft) or so, but this was still insufficient to intercept the U-2, and a further developed MiG-19 featuring a rocket booster was built but was abandoned due to controllability issues as the aircraft tended to enter a supersonic spin. Conventional MiG-19s were involved in several Cold War incidents, including the controversial downing of an RB-47H reconnaissance aircraft in international airspace over the Arctic Circle in July 1960, which resulted in the deaths of four of the crew and two taken prisoner. However, a MiG-19 was lost attempting to intercept Gary Powers' U-2 when it was hit by one of the Soviet SAMs fired at the US aircraft.

Popular export

The MiG-19's impressive performance saw it well received on the export market, and both Czechoslovakia and China obtained licences to produce the aircraft as the Aero S-105 and Shenyang J-6, respectively. One hundred and three S-105s were built, but the Chinese production eventually overtook that of the USSR with some 4500 J-6s, and its F-6 exhort version, produced. Most of the MiG-19s flown in combat against the US by the Vietnamese People's Air Force were, in fact, J-6s, and the type proved effective against faster US aircraft due to its superior manoeuvrability and excellent gun armament. Vietnamese MiG-19/J-6s claimed 13 aircraft shot down for the loss of five MiGs, though the aircraft's short range and comparatively challenging maintenance requirements when compared to the single-engine MiG-17 made it relatively unpopular in service. The Chinese also developed a ground attack variant, the Q-5, which dispensed with the nose intake to allow a targeting radar to be fitted in the nose (though it never was), and around 1300 were built. Shenyang also developed a two-seat trainer, the JJ-6, which was built in large numbers and was retired in China as late as 2019, although it remained in service in small numbers with other nations.

Mikoyan-Gurevich MiG-19P

Weight (maximum take-off): 7730kg (17,042lb)
Dimensions: Length 13.02m (42ft 9in), Wingspan 9m (29ft 6in), Height 3.88m (12ft 9in)
Powerplant: Two Tumansky RD-9B afterburning turbojet engines, each rated at 25.5kN (5700lbf) dry, 31.8kN (7,100lbf) with afterburner
Maximum speed: 1432km/h (890mph)
Range: 1290km (802 miles)
Ceiling: 17,250m (56,594ft)
Crew: 1
Armament: Two 30mm (1.18in) Nudelman-Rikhter NR-30 cannon, fixed, forward firing in wing roots

---

MiG-19P

Though the MiG-19 gave the Cuban air force a supersonic capability, the first of any Latin American air arm. The MiG-19 was unpopular and had only a brief operational life in Cuban hands. The MiG-19Ps were withdrawn in 1966, only four years after entering service.

FIGHTERS

Yakovlev Yak-25 'Flashlight' and 'Mandrake'

The need for a long-range interceptor to protect the Soviet Union's vast territory led to the development of the two-seat Yakovlev Yak-25. The aircraft was also developed into a high-altitude reconnaissance platform with a new straight wing of greater span.

In 1951, design work had begun at the Yakovlev design bureau on a large, twin-engine interceptor featuring a crew consisting of a pilot and a radar intercept operator, the Yak-120. Breaking with previous Yakovlev practice, the design utilized a swept wing with its Mikulin AM-5 turbojets mounted in underwing nacelles. To maximize fuel load yet maintain a suitably thin wing, the Yak-120 employed a bicycle main undercarriage with outriggers under the wingtips, and the aircraft was intended to carry a conformal drop tank on the fuselage centreline for greater range.

The RP-6 'Sokol' intercept radar could detect four-engine bombers at 25km and fighters at around 16km (10 miles) distance and the radar operator seated behind the pilot could fly the aircraft when required due to the aircraft's dual controls, decreasing pilot fatigue on long-duration missions. The aircraft was armed with two 37mm (1.46in) NL-37L cannon, and two 212mm (8.3in) ARS-212 unguided rockets could be carried under the wings.

Flashlight

Flown on 19 June 1952, the Yak-120 exceeded the specified requirements in all aspects except for speed and range but was clearly superior to the rival Lavochkin La-200 and was ordered into production. The first Yak-25s began to come off the assembly line in September 1954, initially fitted with the earlier RP-1 *Izumrud* ('Emerald') radar due to developmental delays afflicting the RP-6.

Once the RP-6 was available, Yakovlev made some other minor changes to the airframe and the improved aircraft was designated the Yak-25M, with deliveries beginning in January 1955. The aircraft became known to the West after being displayed at Tushino in 1955 and was assigned the NATO reporting name 'Flashlight'.

In service, the aircraft proved popular with crews due to its simple flying characteristics and the safety margin its twin-engine configuration afforded on long-distance flights over remote territory. As an interception platform, however, the type was

Yak-25M

The Yak-25M was the most produced variant of the Yak-25 programme, with 406 examples being built. Entering service during 1956, the Yak-25M's service life would prove relatively brief.

Yakovlev Yak-25M

Weight (maximum take-off): 10,045kg (22,145lb)
Dimensions: Length 15.67m (51ft 5in), Wingspan 10.96m (36ft)
Powerplant: Two Mikulin AM-5 turbojet engines, each rated at 19.6kN (4410lbf) thrust
Maximum speed: 1090km/h (677mph)
Range: 2700km (1677 miles)
Ceiling: 12,000m (39,370ft)
Crew: 2
Armament: Two 37mm (1.46in) Nudelman NL-37 cannon fixed, forward firing in two ventral fairings

---

FIGHTERS

A Yak-25 interceptor, photographed in the Central Museum of the Russian Air Force, Monino air base.

somewhat limited, its comparatively low ceiling rendered it unable to intercept the regular incursions by US RB-47 reconnaissance aircraft into Soviet airspace. Its service life was relatively brief, withdrawal began in 1963 and the Yak-25M had disappeared from the frontline inventory by 1967.

Reconnaissance derivative

However, the aircraft's long range and good performance saw it developed as a tactical reconnaissance platform, the Yak-25R, which saw the radar deleted and the second crewman moved to a glazed position in the nose. Only 10 examples of the pre-production Yak-25Rs would be constructed though, as the aircraft was obsolescent by the time it appeared.

A high-altitude reconnaissance derivative, the Yak-25RV, proved considerably more successful though, marrying a single-seat fuselage to a new high aspect ratio straight wing more than double the span of the Yak-25M. Featuring new camera and sensor packs, the Yak-25RV was developed in 1959 and was assigned the reporting name 'Mandrake' by NATO.

Despite its high-altitude capability, the aircraft was difficult to fly at its operating altitude of around 20,000m (65,600ft) because the difference between its maximum speed and the onset of buffeting due to approaching the stall being a mere 10km/h (6mph). Nonetheless, the Yak-25RV soldiered on in service until its replacement by the MiG-25 in the early 1970s.

Yakovlev Yak-25RV

Weight (maximum take-off): 9800kg (21,605lb)
Dimensions: Length 15.93m (52ft 3in), Wingspan 23.4m (76ft 9in), Height 4.3m (14ft 1in)
Powerplant: Two R-11V-300 turbojet engines, each rated at 38.2kN (8598lbf)
Maximum speed: 870km/h (541mph)
Range: 3500km (2175 miles)
Ceiling: 20,500m (67,257ft)
Crew: 1
Armament: None

Yak-25RV

Although difficult to fly, the Yak-25RV with its new straight high aspect ratio wing possessed a unique high altitude reconnaissance capability. These aircraft were much in demand throughout their service lives.

FIGHTERS

Mikoyan-Gurevich MiG-21 'Fishbed'

One of the most significant combat aircraft of the 20th century, the Mikoyan-Gurevich MiG-21 was produced in greater numbers than any other supersonic aircraft. As of 2024, the 'Balalaika' remains in widespread service, some seven decades after its first flight.

Derived from the same aerodynamic work that produced the Su-9, the MiG-21 featured the same tailed-delta configuration but was smaller, lighter and more versatile, though Mikoyan OKB also built a conventional swept-wing version to assess which was the superior design. The first prototype with a delta wing, designated the Ye-4, flew for the first time on 16 June 1955, following the swept-wing Ye-1 and Ye-2, which had flown in February.

Delta wing design

Several more prototypes were built and tested before the delta-wing design was judged to be superior, and the first production aircraft, the MiG-21F (Fishbed-B) with two 30mm (1.18in) cannon, began to be produced in 1959. Just 30 examples of this initial production standard were built before the MiG-21F-13 (Fishbed-C) began to roll off the assembly line in 1960. This aircraft was built in much greater numbers, replacing the limited SRD-5 search radar with the SRD-5M *Kvantum* ('Quantum') set and introducing the ability to carry the AA-2 missile (a copy of the AIM-9 Sidewinder), in addition to the rocket pods and bombs that had previously been all that could be carried by the basic MiG-21F. A bigger tailfin was fitted, and the afterburner was now completely adjustable, but one of the cannon was deleted to save weight. This variant was also the first to be built beyond the Soviet Union, with production undertaken in both Czechoslovakia as the Aero S-106 and China as the Chengdu J-7 and F-7. There followed a bewildering number of variants over the aircraft's 26-year production run too extensive to detail fully here, even discounting non-Soviet versions. The following gives an overview of the production and operational use of the most important of these types.

Second generation

A second-generation MiG-21 was being developed specifically for the air-interception role before the first-generation aircraft had even entered service, and the first development airframe of the new generation, the Ye-7, flew in 1958. Armed solely

MiG-21PF

The first production all-weather interceptor MiG-21 variant, the MiG-21PF began to appear in 1962. This typically anonymous example was serving with the VVS in 1967.

Mikoyan-Gurevich MiG-21PF
Weight (maximum take-off): 9080kg (20,0017lb)
Dimensions: Length 14.1m (46ft 3in), Wingspan 7.15m (23ft 6in), Height 4.71m (15ft 5in)
Powerplant: One Tumansky R-11F2-300 afterburning turbojet rated at 38.7kN (8708lbf) dry, 60.6kN (13,635lbf) with afterburner
Maximum speed: 2175km/h (1351mph)
Range: 1600km (994 miles)
Ceiling: 19,000m (62,336ft)
Crew: 1
Armament: Up to 1000kg (2200lb) of missiles, typically two K-13 or R-ZS air-to-air missiles

27

with missiles, the aircraft featured an uprated engine, larger wheels for better rough-field performance, an enlarged dorsal spine and a wider-diameter forward fuselage so as to house the RP-21M *Sapfir* radar. This variant entered production as the MiG-21P (Fishbed-D) and was replaced on the production lines by the MiG-21PF (Fishbed-F) in 1962, which had a more powerful engine and increased fuel capacity provided by tanks in the dorsal spine.

The MiG-21PF was built in large numbers between 1962 and 1968, both for Soviet use and export, before it was further developed into the MiG-21PFM (Fishbed-F), which had a wider chord tailfin and boundary layer blowing to improve lift and handling at low speeds. Earlier models had been fitted with a one-piece, forward-hinged cockpit canopy designed to tip forward to protect the pilot in the event of an ejection. However, this system never proved entirely satisfactory, and from the PFM model onwards, this changed to a side-hinged canopy with a separate (fixed) windscreen. This was adopted at the same time as the new KM-1 ejection seat, which did not require the canopy to protect the pilot and proved much more reliable than the original SK-1 seat.

The MiG-21PFM became the first Soviet fighter to be built in a non-Communist state when it was adopted for licence production by HAL in India, where it would suffer a truly appalling accident rate (over half the entire fleet have been lost in crashes), leading to the unflattering nickname of 'Flying Coffin'. The MiG-21PFMA (Fishbed-J) saw the introduction of the much more effective RP-22 radar as well as a zero-zero ejection seat and the provision to carry external fuel tanks or a centreline gun pod. A reconnaissance version, the MiG-21R (Fishbed-H), was also developed from the PF. Carrying cameras or electronic surveillance equipment in an underbelly pod, the MiG-21R carried additional fuel and avionics in its dorsal spine and could carry two underwing fuel tanks in place of the single under-fuselage tank carried by fighter versions. The

Czechoslovakia received the MiG-21PFM between 1966 and 1969, flying this variant into the 1990s. Aircraft 4307 was a much photographed example due to its appearance at the Royal International Air Tattoo at Fairford in the UK in 1994.

aircraft could also carry two missiles for self-defence. Large numbers of the MiG-21R were constructed between 1965 and 1971.

First combat

By this point, the MiG-21 had seen combat service, initially in Vietnam, where it proved popular and effective. Exact victory numbers are disputed between the combatants, but what is not in doubt is that the MiG-21 destroyed significant numbers of US aircraft, with the first loss occurring on 7 July 1966 when Tran Ngoc Siu shot down an F-105D. Over the course of the conflict, the VPAF MiG-21s claimed 165 MiG-21 air victories, of which 103 were F-4 Phantoms, for the loss of 65 MiGs. With nine victories, Vietnamese pilot Nguyen Van Coc is acknowledged to be the most successful MiG-21 pilot in history. MiG-21s subsequently saw extensive combat over the Middle East, particularly against Israeli aircraft, in Indian hands against Pakistan and in the various conflicts that have taken place in African states throughout the 1970s and '80s.

Third generation

A third generation of MiG-21 was ushered in with the MiG-21S, which took the increased tankage of the MiG-21R and combined it with the RP-22 radar, along with the ASP-PF-21 computing gunsight, to produce a new tactical fighter variant known to NATO as the Fishbed-H. With four underwing hardpoints, and the two outboard pods being plumbed for drop tanks, this aircraft could carry all the weapons that the MiG-21PFM could but with the addition of the R-3R (K-13R) missile, the semi-active radar homing variant of the K-13.

The MiG-21SM (for *Modernizirovannyy* – 'modernized'), was very similar but reinstated a built-in gun by fitting a GShL-23 23mm (0.9in) cannon as well as introducing a considerably upgraded avionics

Mikoyan-Gurevich MiG-21F-13
Weight (maximum take-off): 8625kg (19,015lb)
Dimensions: Length 13.46m (44ft 2in), Wingspan 7.15m (23ft 6in), Height 4.71m (15ft 5in)
Powerplant: One Tumansky R-13F-300 afterburning turbojet engine rated at 39.9kN (8970lbf) dry, 63.7kN (14320lbf) with afterburner
Maximum speed: 2125km/h (1320mph)
Range: 1600km (994 miles)
Ceiling: 19,000m (62,336ft)
Crew: 1
Armament: One 30mm (1.18in) Nudelman-Rikhter NR-30 cannon fixed forward firing in starboard lower forward fuselage; up to 1000kg (2200lb) of stores, typically two K-13 or K-13A air-to-air missiles

MiG-21F-13
'57 Blue' was one of the first generation models of the MiG-21. At this stage the aircraft was still a comparatively simple, short range lightweight interceptor.

MiG-21F-13
East Germany was one of the first Warsaw Pact nations to receive the MiG-21, this example is equipped, like the Soviet example above, with a supersonic droptank mounted on the centreline pylon.

FIGHTERS

package and new gunsight. The export-only MiG-21M was similar but followed standard Soviet practice in featuring a less powerful engine and downgraded equipment, though this was followed by the MiG-21MF, which was also intended for export but was fitted with a more powerful engine than the MiG-21M, as well as being able to carry a greater variety of weapons, including the R-60 and later the R-60M IR-seeking missiles. This variant was also built in India, with deliveries there beginning in 1973.

MiG-21SMT

One of the MiG-21's primary failings was its short range, and the MiG-21SMT (Fishbed-K) sought to alleviate that issue. Considered the first of the fourth generation MiG-21s and instantly recognizable by its grossly enlarged dorsal spine containing more fuel, this variant was unpopular with pilots due to the significantly degraded handling qualities that ensued. For this reason, most of the MiG-21SMTs were subsequently modified with the dorsal spine of the later MiG-21bis and its smaller tank.

By the 1970s, analysis of Middle Eastern air combat revealed the need for a well-armed low-altitude fighter carrying a large fuel load, and this resulted in the last major MiG-21 variant, the MiG-21bis. Fitted once again with a more powerful engine, the MiG-21bis also featured a much-improved afterburner for enhanced performance above Mach 1. Improved avionics and radar were fitted, and for the first time, the aircraft could demonstrate an all-weather ability.

Two types of MiG-21bis were built, one featuring the *Lazur* GCI system for the PVO squadrons, designated Fishbed-L by NATO, and the VVS version, designated Fishbed-N, which was fitted with the *Polyot* ILS system and a less thirsty R-25 engine. Despite production ending in 1985 (with the exception of China), MiG-21s have seen various upgrades over the years, the most notable of which was probably the Romanian 'LanceR', optimized for ground attack, which entered service in 1997 and was finally withdrawn in 2023.

Trainer version

In addition to the single-seaters, the trainer versions, MiG-21U, US and UM were constructed in quantity, receiving the NATO reporting name 'Mongol'. A grand total of 10,645 MiG-21s were produced in the USSR as well as 840 in India and 194 in Czechoslovakia. Approximately 2400 Chengdu J-7s and F-7s have also been constructed, making the MiG-21 the most produced combat aircraft since the Korean War. Although largely retired, around 10 nations retained operational MiG-21s in 2024.

MiG-21SM

16 Red was serving with the VVS during August 1968 when the Soviet Union invaded Czechoslovakia and wears the tactical red stripe markings on the tail to distinguish Soviet aircraft from the same types in Czech service.

Mikoyan-Gurevich MiG-21SM

Weight (maximum take-off): 9400kg (20,723lb)
Dimensions: Length 14.9m (48ft 11in), Wingspan 7.15m (23ft 6in), Height 4.71m (15ft 5in)
Powerplant: One Tumansky R-13F-300 afterburning turbojet engine rated at 39.9kN (8970lbf) dry, 63.7kN (14320lbf) with afterburner
Maximum speed: 2230km/h (1386mph)
Range: 1420km (882 miles)
Ceiling: 18,000m (59,055ft)
Crew: 1
Armament: One 23mm Gryazev-Shipunov GSh-23L cannon fixed, forward firing in ventral fairing; up to 1300kg (2866lb) bombs, missiles, or stores

Sukhoi Su-9 and Su-11 'Fishpot'

A very fast but short-ranged interceptor, the Sukhoi Su-9 and its Sukhoi Su-11 derivative became the premier Soviet interceptors of the 1960s.

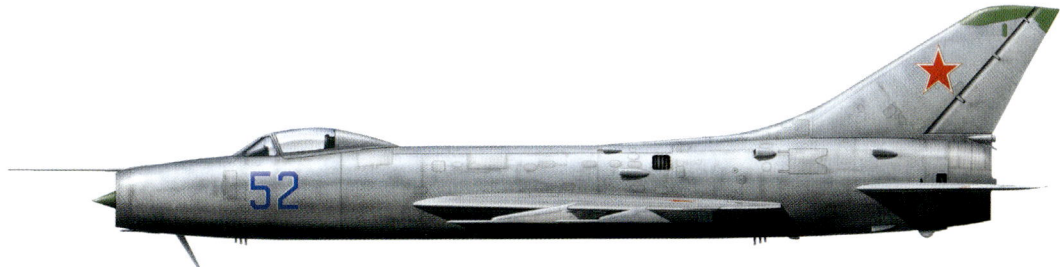

Designed in the early 1950s following a series of aerodynamic studies by the Soviet Central Aerohydrodynamic Institute, Sukhoi's interceptor design featured the same tailed delta layout as the MiG-21 but was a much larger aircraft. Initially, its development was undertaken in parallel with that of the Su-7 Fitter, with its high swept non-delta wing, and following the production of a series of dozens of prototypes and research aircraft, the true prototype of what would become the Su-9, the T-43, took to the air on 10 October 1957. Development work followed, and the aircraft was ordered into production the following year.

The Su-9 was publicly revealed on 9 July 1961 when a formation of Su-9s took part in the air display at Tushino. The aircraft, which was more specialized than the Fitter, was intended as a pure interceptor designed to destroy heavy bombers attacking the Soviet Union. The Su-9 followed contemporary convention and was armed solely with four K-5 beam-riding missiles matched to the R-9 *Sapfir* radar system, and no gun armament was fitted.

Early service use of the Su-9 was problematic and accidents occurred with alarming frequency, mainly due to manufacturing defects of engine and engine accessory components, and the reputation of the aircraft suffered during the first three years of its service life. Much effort was expended to alleviate the issues, and the situation was much improved by 1965.

The performance of the aircraft was undeniably impressive, and the Su-9 would remain the USSR's fastest and highest-flying combat aircraft until the introduction of the MiG-25P Foxbat in 1970. A world absolute altitude record was set by a specially prepared Su-9, designated the T-431, on 14 July 1959 at 28,852m (94,658ft).

Sukhoi Su-11

Further development of the base aircraft resulted in the appearance of the Su-11 (Fishpot-C), which was easily identified from the earlier aircraft by its extended nose, the extra space this afforded being required to house the RP-11 *Oryol* ('Eagle') radar. The long, untapered fuselage led to the Su-11 being nicknamed the 'Flying pipe' by service personnel. A more powerful Lyulka AL-7F-1 turbojet was installed for improved performance at altitude and climb rate, though the Su-11 was a heavier aircraft than its immediate forebear. The beam-riding K-5 missiles

Su-9
Featuring the fuselage of the Su-7 mated to wing design that closely resembles the MiG-21, the Su-9 is commonly misidentified as one or other of these more commonplace aircraft.

Sukhoi Su-9
Weight (maximum take-off): 12,512kg (27,584lb)
Dimensions: Length 16.77m (55ft), Wingspan 8.54m (28ft), Height 4.82m (15ft 10in)
Powerplant: One Lyulka AL-7F-1-100 afterburning turbojet engine, each rated at 66.67kN (14987lbf) thrust dry, 94.12kN (21158lbf) with afterburner
Maximum speed: 2230km/h (1390mph)
Range: 1350km (840 miles)
Ceiling: 20,000m (65,617ft)
Crew: 1
Armament: Up to 500kg (1100lb) of stores, typically four K-5 air-to-air missiles

of the Su-9 were replaced by a pair of R-98 missiles, usually one R-98MR with semi-active radar homing and one R-98MT infrared-guided.

Entering service in 1964, the Su-11 was considered an inferior aircraft to the Su-15 'Flagon' that followed it a mere year or so later, and as a result, production of the Su-11 was curtailed at just over 100 examples, although around 1100 Su-9s had been built. Neither the Su-9 nor the Su-11 was ever exported by the Soviet Union.

FIGHTERS

Tupolev Tu-128 'Fiddler'

The largest and heaviest fighter aircraft ever built, the Tupolev Tu-128 was designed to patrol vast areas of Soviet territory and intercept opposing bomber aircraft such as the Boeing B-52 Stratofortress.

During the 1950s, Soviet planners became increasingly concerned about defending its very long and vulnerable northern border. Contemporary interceptors and surface-to-air missiles were effective but comparatively short-ranged. The supersonic Tu-128 was intended to be able to cover a large area of operations from a few strategic bases; as a result, it was designed to carry a huge fuel load of over 13 tonnes (13.5 tons), allowing for a three-hour endurance and a range of approximately 1560km (970 miles).

Heavy airframe
The aircraft was equipped with the RP-S *Smerch* radar, which possessed a detection range of around 50 km (31 miles) with a lock-on range of about 40km (25 miles). The armament was four R-4 missiles, usually split into a pair of infrared-homing R-4Ts and two R-4Rs with semi-active radar homing. This all required a large, heavy airframe, and the Tu-128, while fast, was not an agile aircraft, though this was of secondary importance to an interceptor that was not normally expected to encounter enemy fighter aircraft.

Tu-28/Tu-128
The Tu-128 made its first public appearance at the 1961 Tushino Air Parade and entered service around four years later. One hundred and ninety eight of these 43-tonne (44 tons) fighters were built, including ten two-seat training aircraft, designated Tu-128UT.

The main production series was originally designated the Tu-28, but this was changed to the Tu-128, identical to Tupolev OKB's internal designation for the aircraft. Generally, though erroneously, it was referred to as the Tu-28 throughout its service life in the West.

Operational aircraft were subject to a modernization programme to improve combat-worthiness at lower altitudes in the late 1970s that saw the new RP-SM *Smerch-M* fitted in combination with R-4RM and R-4TM missiles, although the engines and avionics remained the same. Modernized aircraft were redesignated Tu-128M and remained in frontline service until 1990. The only known 'combat' use of the huge Tu-128 was the destruction of NATO reconnaissance balloons.

Tupolev Tu-128
The original production version of the Tu-128 was known in the West as the Tu-28P, though no such designation existed in the Soviet Union. The enormous Tu-128 was a slow climbing aircraft and its R-4 missiles could be launched up to 8km (5 miles) below its target.

Tu-128
Weight (maximum take-off): 43,700kg (96,342lb)
Dimensions: Length 30.06m (98ft 7in), Wingspan 17.53m (57ft 6in), Height 7.15m (23ft 5in)
Powerplant: Two Lyulka AL-7F-2 afterburning turbojet engines, each rated at 72.8kN (16400lbf) dry, 99.1kN (22300lbf) with afterburner
Maximum speed: 1929km/h (1199mph)
Range: 1560km (970 miles)
Ceiling: 5600m (51,200ft)
Crew: 2
Armament: 6000kg (13230lb) of stores, typically four R-4 long range air-to-air missiles

Sukhoi Su-15 'Flagon'

A highly capable interceptor, the Sukhoi Su-15 represented something of a departure from earlier Sukhoi designs and was intended to address the limitations of the earlier Su-9 and Su-11.

The realization that the Su-9 and Su-11 were ill-equipped to deal with the Boeing B-52 Stratofortress prompted the Sukhoi design bureau to commence development of a significantly more effective interception platform. One of the most pressing requirements was for an improved radar, and this led to the adoption of cheek intakes rather than the nose intake that had been utilized in all previous Sukhoi fighters to enter production.

Nose radome

The new location of the engine intakes freed up the nose area for a large radome containing the Oryol-D ('Eagle') search radar. This was a feature of the Su-9-based T-49 development aircraft, whereas the T-5 was essentially an Su-11 with a widened rear fuselage containing two Tumansky R-11 engines. Combining these two aspects in the same airframe, the T-58 resulted in the prototype Su-15.

The T-58 first flew on 30 May 1962, though the programme was considered important enough that production had already been authorized in February. Service testing commenced the following year, but series production of the Su-15 was delayed somewhat due to insufficient production capacity, the factory assigned to Su-15 construction was busy manufacturing the Yak-28P, and the initial production Su-15s entered service with the PVO in 1967, referred to as Flagon-A by NATO. The aircraft was armed with two R-8/K-8, or later R-98 missiles with either IR or semi-active radar homing. The aircraft was intended to be flown by Ground control datalink until within close proximity to the target, at which point the pilot would take over for final interception.

New wing

Although demonstrating excellent performance in the air, early Su-15s possessed poor take-off and landing characteristics, and a new wing of greater area with extended wingtips and boundary layer control was developed, entering production in 1969. Although there was no change in Soviet designation, aircraft with the new wing

Sukhoi Su-15TM
Weight (maximum take-off): 17,900kg (39,463lb)
Dimensions: : Length 19.56m (64ft 2in), Wingspan 9.43m (30ft 11in), Height 4.84m (15ft 11in)
Powerplant: Two Tumansky R-13F-300 afterburning turbojet engines, each rated at 40.21kN (9040lbf) thrust dry, 70kN (16000lbf) with afterburner
Maximum speed: 2230km/h (1390mph)
Range: 1380km (860 miles)
Ceiling: 18,100m (59,400ft)
Crew: 1
Armament: Up to 1500kg (3300lb) of bombs, rockets, missiles or gunpods

Su-15TM

Fitted with Taifun-M radar and with additional aerodynamic modifications, the Su-15TM was operational from 1971 until 1993 when the Su-15 fleet was abruptly retired to comply with the Treaty on Conventional Armed Forces in Europe.

FIGHTERS

Su-15

When introduced, the Su-15 delivered a considerable jump in capability over the aircraft it replaced. Although it had much the same maximum speed as the Su-11 for example, the Su-15 boasted nearly double the climb rate with superior radar and armament.

were named Flagon-D by NATO. The new wing also allowed four missiles to be carried. A two-seat training variant was developed during this period, the Su-15UT (Flagon-C), featuring no radar or combat capability. The year 1969 also saw the upgraded Su-15T with Volkov *Taifun* ('Typhoon') radar enter testing, but this proved troublesome, and production was curtailed after only ten aircraft had been built.

Su-15TM

By December 1971, however, the Su-15TM (Flagon-E) had appeared, with the improved Taifun-M radar and provision for UPK-23-250 gun pod or R-60 short-range air-to-air missiles. A redesign of the radome with an ogival shape again led to a new NATO reporting name, Flagon-F, while the Soviet designation remained unchanged, and a combat-capable trainer, the Su-15UM (Flagon-G), entered service in 1976. Production continued until 1979.

The operational service life of the Su-15 was quite long, with the aircraft remaining in frontline service from 1965 to 1993 (1996 in Ukraine), and the aircraft was never exported, serving only with the Soviet Union and its successor states of Russia and Ukraine.

Although the Su-15 never engaged an enemy bomber, it was involved in several interceptions of civil aircraft that had strayed into Soviet territory, most infamously a Korean Air Lines Boeing 747 in 1983, which resulted in the deaths of all 269 people on board.

Sukhoi Su-15

Weight (maximum take-off): 17,094kg (37,686lb)
Dimensions: Length 22.07m (72ft 5in), Wingspan 8.62m (28ft 3in), Height 5m (16ft 5in)
Powerplant: Two Tumansky R-11F2S-300 afterburning turbojet engines, each rated at 38.7kN (8708lbf) dry, 60.6kN (13635lbf) with afterburner
Maximum speed: 2230km/h (1390mph)
Range: 1550km (963 miles)
Ceiling: 18,500m (60,696ft)
Crew: 1
Armament: Two R-8 or R-98 air-to-air missiles

Mikoyan-Gurevich MiG-25 'Foxbat'

A staggeringly fast aircraft, the Mikoyan-Gurevich MiG-25 initially caused considerable consternation in the West. The MiG-25 saw extensive combat during the Iran–Iraq War and served for many years with India.

During the late 1950s, the B-70 Valkyrie appeared to be about to give the US a Mach-3 capable bomber that Soviet aircraft would be unable to intercept. This, combined with the high-altitude incursions of the U-2, led to the development of a new interceptor with the speed and altitude performance necessary to deal with any potential threat, the MiG-25. Work began in earnest on the MiG-25 in 1959, and the aircraft made its maiden flight on 6 March 1964, initially fitted with two large wingtip fuel tanks, though these were soon discarded. Performance was spectacular, and three prototypes were utilized to set 29 world records,

Mikoyan-Gurevich MiG-25RBM
Weight (maximum take-off): 41,200kg (90,830lb)
Dimensions: Length 22.27m (73ft 1in), Wingspan 13.42m (44ft), Height 6m (19ft 8in)
Powerplant: Two Tumansky R-15B-300 afterburning turbojet engines, each rated at 73.5kN (16500lbf) thrust dry, 100.1kN (22500lbf) with afterburner
Maximum speed: 3000km/h (1865mph)
Range: 1860km (1156 miles)
Ceiling: 23,000m (75,460ft)
Crew: 1
Armament: Up to 5000kg (11,023lb) stores

MiG-25RBM

Fewer than 100 of the MiG-25RBM variant are believed to have been produced for the suppression of enemy air defence role. Produced between 1982 and 1986, this variant served with VVS units in Poland and East Germany but was never exported.

FIGHTERS

including the absolute altitude record for a jet aircraft at 37,650m (123,520ft). Several of the records set by the MiG-25, including this one, still stand. The aircraft's great speed resulted in high temperatures being generated due to friction with the air, and this meant that virtually all of the airframe was constructed of nickel steel, which has great thermal resistance but is very heavy.

Reconnaissance variant
The first MiG-25 variant to enter production was the reconnaissance variant, the MiG-25R (Foxbat-B), which started to be produced in 1969. In 1971, this was followed by the MiG-25P Foxbat-A interceptor with RP-25 Smerch-A1 ('Tornado') radar and four large R-40 missiles available with semi-active radar homing or infrared homing. The Foxbat-C was the NATO designation given to the unarmed two-seat training variant. Initial service use saw the MiG-25R transferred to Egypt to perform overflights over Israel, and one of these aircraft was tracked over Sinai travelling at Mach 3.2 (though flying at this speed irreparably damaged the engines). Interceptor Foxbats remained within the confines of the USSR until, sensationally, Lieutenant Viktor Belenko defected to Japan in his MiG-25P interceptor, allowing Western experts their first look at such an aircraft.

MiG-25PD
Although Belenko's Foxbat was returned to the Soviet Union, the radar and missile systems were obviously now compromised, and an updated interceptor variant, the MiG-25PD (Foxbat-E) was developed after 1976.

Missiles
The Bisnovat R-40, known to NATO as the AA-6 'Acrid', was specifically designed for use with the MiG-25 and its Smerch-A (Tornado-A) radar. '31 Red' is carrying two radar homing R-40R and two infrared homing R-40T missiles, as was standard Soviet practice.

FIGHTERS

Featuring a new *Sapfir*-25 radar supplemented by an IRST system and the ability to carry R-60 missiles, the MiG-25PD was in production from 1978 to 1984, and earlier airframes were modified to the same standard. Another result of the defection was that export of the MiG-25 was permitted for the first time due to the basic design no longer being secret, and six nations ultimately placed orders for Foxbats.

It was in the hands of the Iraqi Air Force that the MiG-25 would undertake its most intense operational service, with MiG-25s credited with the destruction of at least 15 Iranian aircraft, including F-4 Phantoms and one F-14 Tomcat. India was also a major user of the MiG-25, although in contrast to Iraq, India's Foxbats were all reconnaissance models. The aircraft was heavily employed during the Kargil War of 1999 and Operation Parakram in 2001–2 to conduct aerial reconnaissance over Pakistan. By 2024, virtually all MiG-25s had been retired, but two MiG-25Rs were known to be in service with the Syrian Air Force at the start of 2023, and these may still be operational. The last interceptor Foxbats were retired in July 2022 when Algeria withdrew its last remaining MiG-25Ps.

Radar
The Foxbat's Smerch-A radar weighed half a tonne and was extremely powerful, conferring a high resistance to ECM countermeasures. It was estimated that it would acquire a XB-70 sized target at 90km (56 miles), giving the pilot 60 seconds to intercept at the high speeds both aircraft were intended to operate at.

Engines
The MiG-25's maximum speed was limited to Mach 2.83. The Tumansky R-15 engines could propel the aircraft faster but tend to overspeed and overheat at higher speeds. In 1971 a MiG-25 was tracked flying over Sinai at Mach 3.2, but the engines were so damaged by flying at this speed that the aircraft was scrapped.

Mikoyan-Gurevich MiG-25P
Weight (maximum take-off): 90,390lb (41,000kg)
Dimensions: Length 22.3m (73ft 2in), Wingspan 14.06m (46ft 2in), Height 6.5m (21ft 4in)
Powerplant: Two Tumansky R-15B-300 afterburning turbojet engines, each rated at 73.5kN (16500lbf) thrust dry, 100.1kN (22,500lbf) with afterburner
Maximum speed: 3000km/h (1865mph)
Range: 1860km (1160 miles)
Ceiling: 24,000m (78,740ft)
Crew: 1
Armament: Up to 4000kg (8818lb) stores, typically four R-40T or R-40R air-to-air missiles

MiG-25P

'31 Red' was the aircraft in which Victor Belenko defected to Japan in September 1976. Western powers were under the impression that the Foxbat was a highly manoeuvrable fighter in the same class as the F-15, then under development. The temporary acquisition of Belenko's MiG-25 revealed the true nature of the aircraft: formidable but specialised.

FIGHTERS

Mikoyan-Gurevich MiG-23 'Flogger'

With over 5000 built, the Mikoyan-Gurevich MiG-23 has become the most produced variable geometry aircraft in history. After overcoming initial teething problems, it matured into a highly capable fighter and interceptor.

Developed as a replacement for the MiG-21, the new aircraft was intended to improve on performance, range and take-off performance whilst carrying more capable avionics and weapons, including BVR missiles. By contrast, manoeuvrability was not considered of prime importance. To maximize its short take-off ability, MiG experimented with lift jets in the fuselage but instead focused on a variable geometry wing, which could be swept to settings of 16, 45 and 72 degrees. First flown as the Ye-231 on 10 June 1967, the first production aircraft took to the air on 21 May 1969, designated the MiG-23S (Flogger-A to NATO).

Early MiG-23s were subject to numerous flight restrictions due to significant teething issues and were not popular with pilots, who found that the new fighter was unable to outmanoeuvre the MiG-21. Not only that but as the Sapfir-23 ('Sapphire') radar had been delayed, it was equipped with the earlier RP-22SM Sapfir radar and was not equipped with an IRST. Notable faults included dangerous handling at high angles of attack, a propensity to enter a spin and the discovery of cracks in the joints between the fuselage and wings.

Several fatal accidents occurred, and only around 60 MiG-23S aircraft were produced before production switched to the improved MiG-23 (with no suffix). This was equipped with the Sapfir-23 radar, though this proved unreliable in service, and featured some changes to the airframe. The tail surfaces were moved rearwards 86cm (34in) and new wings of increased area were fitted, requiring changed wing sweep settings. The wings, though simpler to manufacture, actually worsened the handling, so only approximately 80 MiG-23s were built before the introduction of the considerably superior MiG-23M Flogger-B.

The Flogger-B became the most produced of the first-generation MiG-23s, with approximately 1300 being constructed between 1972 and 1978, and by the late 1970s, the MiG-23M had become the Soviet Union's premier air-superiority fighter. Apart from the very first examples, the MiG-23M featured the Sapfir-23D, allowing 'look-down/shoot-down' capability for

MiG-23M
'66 Red' is an example of the first mass-produced variant, the MiG-23M Flogger-B. Plumbed pylons were introduced to allow the MiG-23M to carry 800 litre drop tanks when the wings were at full spread but this example carries only rocket launchers.

Mikoyan-Gurevich MiG-23MF
Weight (maximum take-off): 18,400kg (40,565lb)
Dimensions: Length 16.7m (54ft 9in), Wingspan 13.97m (45ft 10in) wings spread, 7.78m (25ft 10in) wings fully-swept, Height 4.82m (15ft 10in)
Powerplant: One Tumansky R-29-300 afterburning turbojet engine rated at 78.48kN (17,640lbf) dry, 112.81kN (25360lbf) with afterburner
Maximum speed: 2500km/h (1553mph)
Range: 1450km (900 miles)
Ceiling: 17,500m (57,415ft)
Crew: 1
Armament: One 23mm (0.91in) Gryazev-Shipunov GSh-23L twin-barrelled Gast cannon fixed forward firing in lower forward fuselage; up to 2000kg (4400lb) of bombs, missiles, or stores

---

38

FIGHTERS

the first time with its R-23 and R-60 missiles. The aircraft also benefited from an improved flight control system, autopilot and navigation system. The wing was updated to its definitive form, the so-called Edition-3 wing, delivering better handling, although wing-sweep problems initially resulted in a 5G limit on the airframe. The MiG-23MF was produced as an export variant to other Warsaw Pact states with different IFF and communication equipment, as well as the comprehensively downgraded MiG-23MS, intended for supply to third-world nations.

MiG-23ML

Further development resulted in the MiG-23ML, and externally identical MLA, Flogger-G, which saw combat effectiveness increased by around 20 per cent according to MiG. The airframe was both lightened and strengthened and was now rated for subsonic manoeuvres up to 8.5G, and 7.5G supersonic. Performance, manoeuvrability and reliability were improved, and provision was now made for the underwing pylons to accommodate UPK-23-250 23mm (0.9in) gun pods.

The ultimate MiG-23 fighter model was the Flogger-K MiG-23MLD, which differed mainly in featuring aerodynamic changes to improve the aircraft's manoeuvrability at high angles of attack. The MLD also incorporated improved avionics, some developed for the MiG-29 to improve handling

and safety. The Sapfir-23MLA-II radar offered greater range, reliability, resistance to enemy countermeasures and improved look-down/shoot/down capability, as well as a separate close range dogfighting mode. No new-build MiG-23MLDs were constructed for the VVS but were all conversions of existing airframes, though some new-build aircraft were constructed for export – the last of these was supplied to Syria in 1984, becoming the final MiG-23s of any subtype to be built.

MiG-23B and MiG-23P

Two further lines of development saw the production of the MiG-23B Flogger-F, optimized for the ground attack role, which would evolve into the MiG-27, described in detail in chapter 2, and the MiG-23P, Flogger-L, a dedicated interceptor variant for the PVO defence units. This aircraft was developed essentially as a stopgap to replace the ageing Su-9 and Su-11s still in service, offering the necessary performance and capability to deal with modern threats, such as the F-111. Like other PVO aircraft, the MiG-23P was intended to be flown under ground control to its target, using the SAU-23P autopilot in conjunction with the Lasur-M datalink, with the pilot controlling only the engine and weapons.

Around 500 MiG-23Ps were built, becoming the most numerous interceptors in PVO service in the 1980s, and they were considered

formidable, especially in BVR combat. The aircraft survived in service beyond the end of the Soviet Union with Russian units, with the last being retired in 1998.

As with other Soviet fighters, many two-seat trainers were built as the MiG-23U and the MiG-23UB (both named Flogger-C by NATO), both combat capable, though later production MiG-23UBs dispensed with the Sapfir-21M radar originally fitted and replaced it with ballast. Just over 1000 Flogger-Cs were constructed.

Mikoyan-Gurevich MiG-23MLD

Weight (maximum take-off): 17,800kg (39,242lb)
Dimensions: Length 16.7m (54ft 9in) Wingspan 13.97m (45ft 10in) wings spread, 7.78m (25ft 10in) wings fully-swept, Height 4.82m (15ft 10in)
Powerplant: One Khatchaturov R-35-300 afterburning turbojet engine, rated at 83.6kN (18,800lbf) dry, 127.49kN (28660lbf) with afterburner
Maximum speed: 2500km/h (1600mph)
Range: 1450km (900 miles)
Ceiling: 18,500m (60,700ft)
Crew: 1
Armament: One 23mm (0.91in) Gryazev-Shipunov GSh-23L twin-barrelled Gast cannon fixed forward firing in lower forward fuselage; up to 2000kg (4400lb) of bombs, missiles, or stores

MiG-23MLD

Pictured as it appeared in 1986 when on operational service in Afghanistan, this MiG-23MLD is finished in typical Soviet camouflage adopted for tactical aircraft. The MiG-23MLD (Flogger-K in the West) was the ultimate MiG-23 fighter variant.

FIGHTERS

Yakovlev Yak-38 'Forger'

Developed for service on the Soviet Navy's Kiev class carriers, the Yakovlev Yak-38 was the Soviet Union's only VTOL strike fighter aircraft to see service as well as being its first operational carrier-based fixed-wing aircraft.

The Yakovlev design bureau had developed the land-based Yak-36 VTOL fighter aircraft during the 1960s, and though it never entered production, this supplied a wealth of data and experience that could be utilized in the Yak-38. Yakovlev had wished to pursue a design similar to the Hawker Harrier, with vectored thrust supporting the aircraft in the hover, but the lack of a suitably powerful engine forced the Yak-38 to utilize two lifting jet engines in the forward fuselage, used purely for landing and take-off, combined with the vectored thrust of the main engine. The available power was marginal, and engine failure in vertical flight was a serious enough concern for the Yak-38 to be fitted with an automatic ejection seat; if one of the engines failed or the

Yak-38M

Due to the propensity of the blue scheme to fade prematurely, later production aircraft were finished in this two-tone grey scheme. Like the aircraft above, this airframe is also preserved at the Ukraine State Aviation Museum in Kyiv.

Yak-38M

Initially, Yak-38s were finished in this attractive dark blue scheme with green undersides and most photographs of operational Forgers feature aircraft in these colours. Today, this aircraft is preserved at the Ukraine State Aviation Museum.

aircraft rolled past 60 degrees, the pilot was automatically ejected.

The aircraft was flown for the first time on 15 January 1971 in its pre-production form as the Yak-36M. This designation was initially retained even though the new aircraft had nothing in common with the earlier Yak-36. Much development work was required before the definitive Yak-38 aircraft eventually entered service in August 1976. Aboard the Kiev class carriers, an air wing of 12 Yak-38s was usually carried, and the aircraft served until its withdrawal in 1992. One-hundred-and-forty-three examples of the initial production variant Yak-38 were built followed by 50 of an upgraded version, the Yak-38M, which featured more powerful engines that allowed for operations at

greater weights. Thirty-eight examples of the two-seat training variant, the Yak-38U, were also constructed. Development of a far more capable supersonic successor to the Yak-38, the Yak-141 'Freestyle', saw four prototypes constructed, but funding was withdrawn following the collapse of the Soviet Union, and the aircraft never entered production.

Yakovlev Yak-38M

Weight (maximum take-off): 11,300kg (24,912lb)
Dimensions: Length 16.37m (53ft 8in), Wingspan 7.32m (24ft), Height 4.25m (13ft 11in)
Powerplant: One Tumansky R-28 V-300 Vectored-thrust turbofan engine, rated at 66.7kN (15,000lbf) thrust and two Rybinsk (RKBM) RD-38 turbojet engines, each rated at 31.9kN (7200lbf) thrust
Maximum speed: 1050km/h (650mph)
Range: 1300km (810 miles)
Ceiling: 11,000m (36,000ft)
Crew: 1
Armament: Up to 2000kg (4400lb) of bombs, missiles, or stores

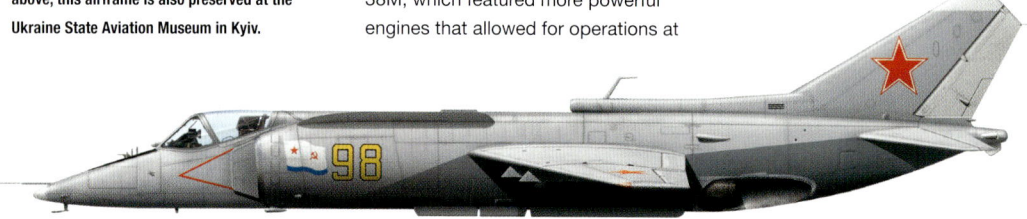

Mikoyan-Gurevich MiG-31 'Foxhound'

A long-range interceptor derived from the Mikoyan-Gurevich MiG-25, the Mikoyan-Gurevich MiG-31 entered service in the early 1980s and remains one of the world's fastest aircraft. It is expected to remain operational until at least 2030.

Originally, this aircraft was schemed in 1968 as a long-range, Mach 2.8 interceptor and was initially considered a straightforward two-seat MiG-25 variant, designated MiG-25MP, featuring a multi-target capability and better endurance. However, the programme evolved into the heavily redesigned MiG-31. The first flight of the MIG-25MP took place on 16 September 1975, and the initial production MiG-31 appeared in late 1976.

Phased-array fighter radar

The MiG-31 entered service with the Soviet Air Defence Forces in May 1981, and early production aircraft featured the *Zaslon* fire-control system, the world's first operational electronically scanned phased-array fighter radar. Carrying four semi-active radar-guided R-33 or R-33S air-to-air missiles in pairs under the fuselage, as well as two medium-range infrared-guided R-40TD or four infrared-guided R-60M air-to-air missiles on the wing pylons for self-defence, four MiG-31s were intended between them to be capable of defending airspace along a front of around 800–900km (500–560 miles). Boasting almost double the range of the MiG-25 and a far more capable sensor suite and weapons array than the Tu-128, the MiG-31 replaced both aircraft in the long-range interceptor role. The aircraft was intended to protect the northern and far eastern borders of the USSR and was specifically designed to defend against cruise missile attack as part of a ground-controlled intercept (GCI) network (though it is also fully capable of operating autonomously).

The advanced MiG-31M Foxhound-B interceptor and the anti-satellite MiG-31D were developed in the 1980s. However, they were cancelled in the early 1990s when military funding collapsed following the end of the Soviet Union. Today, around 130 aircraft remain in service in Russia, with approximately the same number in storage.

MiG-31M

The higher loaded weight of the MiG-31 necessitated the use of a landing bogie in place of the single-wheel main undercarriage units as fitted to the MiG-25 from which the Foxhound was derived. The finned wingtip pod houses ECM equipment.

Mikoyan-Gurevich MiG-31M
Weight (maximum take-off): 46,200kg (101,854lb)
Dimensions: Length 22.62m (74ft 3in), Wingspan 13.46m (44ft 2in), Height 6.46m (21ft 2in)
Powerplant: Two Soloviev D-30F6 afterburning turbofan engines, each rated at 93kN (21,000lbf) dry, 152kN (34,000lbf) with afterburner
Maximum speed: 3000km/h (1865mph)
Range: 3000km (1865 miles)
Ceiling: 25,000m (82,000ft)
Crew: 2
Armament: One 23mm (0.91in) Gryazev-Shipunov GSh-6-23M rotary cannon fixed forward firing above starboard landing gear well, up to 3000kg (6600lb) of stores, typically four R-33 long range air-to-air missiles, or two R-40T medium range and four R-60 short range air-to-air missiles

FIGHTERS

Sukhoi Su-27 'Flanker'

Arguably the most capable Soviet fighter to be developed before the end of the Cold War, the Sukhoi Su-27 was designed as a counter to the USAF's F-15 and remains in service today in several nations.

Su-27K
The Su-27K was still in development as the Soviet Union collapsed, but managed to survive the savage cutbacks of the immediate post-Soviet era; a developed version of the aircraft entered service in the mid-1990s as the Su-33.

Designed as a 'heavy' long-range air-superiority fighter and escort fighter to complement the 'light' MiG-29, Su-27 development began as the *Perspektivnyi Frontovoi Istrebitel*, or Future Tactical Fighter programme, which was initiated in 1969 in response to the development of the McDonnell Douglas F-15.

Sukhoi's T-10 design was selected in 1971, and the first prototype T-10-1 made its maiden flight on 20 May 1977, slightly less than five years after the first flight of the F-15. Seven T-10s (Flanker-A) were constructed, and the testing process was protracted due to various problems, particularly with the fly-by-wire system, resulting in two fatal crashes. The design was thoroughly revised during this period, resulting in the T-10S, the first prototype of which made its maiden flight on 20 April 1981.

Radar
Developed by the Tikhomirov Scientific Research Institute of Instrument Design specifically for use in the Su-27 the N001 Mech (Sword) radar initially proved very disappointing. Nonetheless the radar managed to scrape through its State trials and was fitted to the Su-27 mainly because there was no alternative set available. It was subsequently much improved in the post-Soviet era.

Cockpit
The Su-27 featured more analogue instrumentation than its Western contemporaries but Flanker pilots had a decisive advantage over their NATO rivals in their helmet mounted sight which allowed them to aim and fire missiles within a wide hemisphere in front of the aircraft; a feature unavailable to US pilots until 2003 and potentially devastating in close-in combat.

Su-27S
Based in Poland, '48 Blue' was serving with the 582 Fighter Aviation Regiment at Chojna Airbase in 1992. Su-27 units 582 IAP and 159 GvIAP would pull out of Poland in the same year following the dissolution of the Soviet Union.

Production

Production aircraft began to appear from June 1982 and were supplied in two basic forms: the initial Su-27, which was quickly supplanted by the Su-27S with an improved AL-31F engine, and the Su-27P air defence version, which was produced for the Soviet Air Defence Forces. The latter aircraft dispensed with the air-to-ground capability of the basic Su-27, though both types were known as Flanker-B to NATO. Series production of single-seaters was followed in 1986 by the two-seat Su-27UB combat trainer

Sukhoi Su-27S
Weight (maximum take-off): 33,000kg (72,751lb)
Dimensions: Length Length 21.9m (71ft 10in), Wingspan 14.7m (48ft 3in), Height 5.9m (19ft 5in)
Powerplant: Two Saturn AL-31F afterburning turbofan engines each rated at 79.43kN (17,857lbf) dry and 122.58kN (27,557lbf) with afterburner
Maximum speed: 2280km/h (1417mph)
Range: 3680km (2287 miles)
Ceiling: 17,700m (58,071ft)
Crew: 1
Armament: One 30mm (1.18in) Gryazev-Shipunov GSh-30-1 cannon fixed forward firing in starboard leading edge extension; up to 6000kg of bombs, missiles, or stores

(Flanker-C) with the same fire-control system and weapons but reduced fuel capacity. A lightened version appeared in 1986, designated the P-42, with engines modified to deliver an increase in thrust of 1000kg (2200lb), which successfully beat the time-to-height records set by the F-15 'Streak Eagle', several of which still stand.

Initial operational capability was declared on the type in December 1984, though production delays meant that the aircraft never achieved its planned strength until 1990. Just before the Cold War ended, the naval Flanker derivative, the Su-27K (Flanker-D), entered service. Carrier qualification took place in November 1989 aboard the carrier *Admiral Kuznetsov*, then named *Tblisi* and carrier operations commenced in September 1991, some three months before the collapse of the Soviet Union.

Post-Cold War strength

The demise of the USSR left Su-27s in the hands of Belarus (now retired), Ukraine and Uzbekistan, as well as Russia, where the aircraft became the most important fighter type. Though the Su-27 has been superseded to some degree, as of 2024, the Russian Aerospace Forces still retained around 100 Sukhoi Su-27s on strength, complemented by approximately 20 trainers.

Su-27 development would, of course, continue in Russia beyond the end of the Cold War to produce the two-seat multirole Su-30, the Naval Su-33, the Su-34 strike aircraft and the improved Su-35 air superiority single-seater. The Su-27 has been licence-built in China – which was also the first export customer back in 1992 – as the J-11.

Approximately 680 examples of the Su-27 were built in the USSR and Russia as well as a further 440 J-11s in China, and first-generation Flankers still form part of the frontline inventory of around ten nations, though all of these have seen various upgrades and modernization programmes.

Tailfin
On the T-10 prototype, the two large vertical tailfins were mounted on top of the engine nacelles but on production Su-27s, they had were moved to their definitive position outboard of the engines.

FIGHTERS

Mikoyan MiG-29 'Fulcrum'

The supremely agile Mikoyan MiG-29 caused something of a stir in Western circles when East Germany's MiG-29 fleet became a part of NATO following Germany's reunification. The aircraft remains a highly capable and versatile fighter in widespread service around the globe.

During the early 1970s, the Soviet Union developed a 'light' fighter project to complement the 'heavy' Su-27, and intended primarily to function as an air-superiority fighter. The *Perspektivnyy Lyogkiy Frontovoy Istrebitel* (LPFI, or 'Advanced Lightweight Tactical Fighter') programme mirrored the development of the F-16 in the USA – both aircraft were the result of efforts to limit the seemingly inexorable growth in weight and complexity of modern fighters. The first flight of the MiG-29 took place on 6 October 1977, and after 14 development aircraft were built, the first pre-series aircraft flew in early 1979, followed by production aircraft in the summer of 1982.

The MiG-29 was officially commissioned into service in 1987 after various improvements had been made, but it had actually first become operational in 1980, with a detachment of aircraft being based at Wittstock, East Germany, in 1986. Initial production standard aircraft were referred to as Fulcrum-A by NATO. This was followed by the improved single-seat Fulcrum-C version (there was no distinction made between these versions in Soviet service), which featured additional internal fuel capacity as well as provision for two 1150L (253 gal) drop tanks under the wings. This was in addition to the standard 1500L (330 gal) auxiliary under-fuselage fuel tank. A new Gardenia electronic jammer

MiG-29

During July 1986, '03 Blue' was one of six early production MiG-29s visiting Kuopio-Russala Air Base in Finland as part of a squadron exchange with MiG-21 unit HavLv 31. The MiG-29s were part of the 234th Guards Fighter Aviation Regiment, based at Kubinka.

MiG-29

An early production MiG-29 launches an R-73 missile. Known to NATO as the AA-11 Archer, the R-73 possessed a better performance than AIM-9 Sidewinders in the late 1980s and it formed a formidable combination with the highly manoeuvrable MiG-29.

44

MiG-29S

Based at Falkenburg, East Germany in 1991, '33 Red' was on the strength of the 31st Guards Fighter Regiment, subordinated to 6th Guards Fighter Aviation Division.

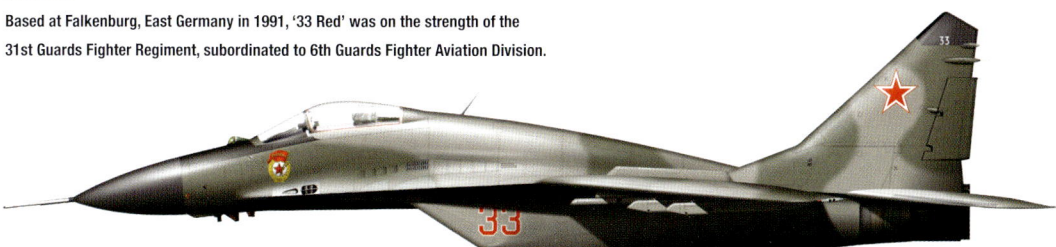

was fitted in the bulged fuselage spine. The armament consisted of two medium-range R-27R air-to-air missiles with semi-active radar guidance carried on the inner pylons, with four short-range R-73 or R-60M air-to-air missiles with infrared guidance on the outer pylons. Alternatively, up to 4000kg (8818lb) of offensive stores on the same six pylons, including tactical nuclear bombs, freefall conventional bombs, napalm tanks, sub-munitions dispensers and various unguided rockets, could be carried.

A two-seat MiG-29UB (Fulcrum-B) version was developed, which featured an additional seat in front of the pilot's position and a slightly extended fuselage. The radar was deleted on the two-seater, but IRST, cannon and weapons pylons were all retained. The last version to appear in the Soviet era was the MiG-29S, an advanced version of the Fulcrum-C with a modernized N019M Topaz radar of increased range, as well the capability for R-77, R-27T and R-27RE/TE missiles.

Modern upgrades

The MiG-29S flew in 1990, but the collapse of the Soviet Union saw only a small batch produced for domestic service. Large-scale production ceased in 1993 after 1345 production aircraft had been built. However, with a large number of unfinished aircraft left at the factories, small-scale production continued after this date, including a few new-build aircraft. Like the Su-27, the MiG-29 has been subject to many subsequent upgrades: most Russian examples are now of the MiG-29SMT variant, with many internal improvements and greater fuel load carried in a much-enlarged spine, and the basic airframe has been developed into both the MiG-29K carrier variant and MiG-35 upgraded version.

The MiG-29 remains in service with over 20 nations, most of which have been subject to upgrades to improve their multirole capabilities, and the Russian Aerospace Force retains around 150 single-seaters and approximately 30 two-seaters on strength.

Mikoyan MiG-29S

Weight (maximum take-off): 19,700kg (42,680lb)
Dimensions: Length 17.32m (56ft 10in), Wingspan 11.36m (37 ft 3in), Height 4.73m (15ft 6in)
Powerplant: Two Klimov RD-33 afterburning turbofan engines each rated at 49.42kN (11,110lbf) dry and 81.39kN (18298lbf) with afterburner
Maximum speed: 2445km/h (1519mph)
Range (with external tanks): 1500km (932 miles)
Ceiling: 17,000m (55,775ft)
Crew: 1
Armament: One 30mm (1.18in) Gryazev-Shipunov GSh-30-1 cannon fixed forward firing in starboard leading edge extension; up to 4000kg (8818lb) of bombs, missiles, or stores

ATTACK AIRCRAFT

With its historical reputation as a tactical adjunct to the Red Army, it comes as no surprise that the VVS operated a selection of highly effective fighter-bomber and dedicated attack aircraft. Mirroring developments in the West, ground attack aircraft were very fast derivatives of supersonic fighters in the 1950s and 60s before returning to purpose-designed, comparatively slow aircraft in the 1970s and 80s.

The following aircraft are included in this chapter:

- Ilyushin Il-10 'Beast'
- Sukhoi Su-7 'Fitter'
- Sukhoi Su-17 and Sukhoi Su-22 'Fitter'
- Sukhoi Su-24 'Fencer'
- Mikoyan-Gurevich MiG-27 'Flogger'
- Sukhoi Su-25 'Frogfoot'

Famed for its excellent handling and one of the most successful aircraft developed in the latter stages of the Cold War, the Su-25 remains in full combat service with a variety of air arms.

ATTACK AIRCRAFT

Ilyushin Il-10 'Beast'

Designed during World War II as a replacement for the iconic Il-2 Sturmovik, the Il-10 appeared too late to see major service during that conflict but served for many years into the Cold War.

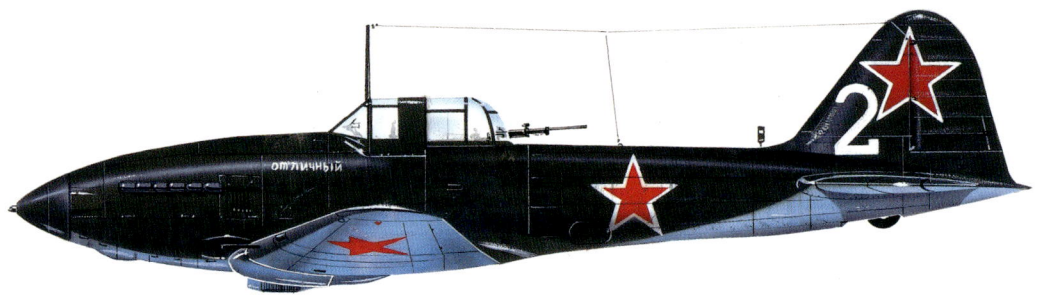

Derived from a proposal for a single-seat, heavily armoured fighter intended to attack bombers and transports, Ilyushin altered the design as a two-seat ground attack aircraft to replace the Il-2 when the fighter project was abandoned. The Il-10 beat two other contenders in trials, a second Ilyushin design, the Il-8, as well as the rival, radial-engined Sukhoi Su-6, and was ordered into production in August 1944.

Heavily armoured
The Il-10 featured the same powerful armament and followed the same successful concept of a heavily armoured airframe as the earlier Il-2. Powered by a more powerful 1320kW (1770hp) Mikulin AM-42 and possessing a smaller airframe, the Il-10 proved to be 145km/h (90mph) faster than the older aircraft and demonstrated excellent manoeuvrability.

The aircraft entered service in January 1945 and was in action from 15 April 1945 until VE day less than a month later and attacked rail and

Il-10
Clearly displaying its World War II origins, the Il-10 offered a useful improvement to the capabilities of the famed Il-2 but was built in much smaller numbers.

shipping targets in the brief Soviet campaign against Japan in the summer of 1945. The Il-10 saw further combat during the Korean War, initially with considerable success against the poorly equipped South Korean forces, but the Il-10 struggled against modern fighters, and few were left by the late summer of 1950.

Built under licence
In production until 1954 in the USSR, the Il-10 was also built under licence in Czechoslovakia, as the Avia B-33, until 1956. Later models featured a heavier armament of four 23mm (0.9in) Nudelman-Suranov NS-23 cannon with a 20mm (0.79in) Berezin B-20 cannon for the rear gunner. The last operational Il-10s were retired by China in 1972 and replaced by the supersonic Nanchang Q-5.

Ilyushin Il-10
Weight (maximum take-off): 6535kg (14,407lb)
Dimensions: Length: 11.06m (36ft 3in), Wingspan: 13.40m (43ft 11in), Height: 4.18m (13ft 9in)
Powerplant: One 1320kW (1770hp) Mikulin AM-42 V12 liquid-cooled piston engine
Maximum speed: 551km/h (342mph)
Range: 800km (500 miles)
Ceiling: 5500m (18,000ft)
Crew: 2
Armament: Two 23mm (0.91in) Vya-23 cannon and two 7.62mm (0.3in) ShKAS machine guns fixed forward firing in wing, one 20mm (0.79in) Berezin B-20 cannon or one 12.7mm (0.5in) Berezin UBT machine gun flexibly mounted in rear turret, up to 600kg (1320lb) of bombs or unguided rockets

Sukhoi Su-7 'Fitter'

Rugged, simple and very fast, but short-ranged and limited in payload, the supersonic Su-7 was the Soviet Union's primary fighter bomber during the 1960s.

Sukhoi began work on two parallel designs in 1953, one with a delta wing (that would eventually mature into the Su-9 interceptor) and a second with a highly swept wing, originally designated the S-1. Flown on 8 September 1955, the S-1 proved to be extremely fast, achieving a level speed of 2170km/h (1350mph) in April 1956. This was faster than any other Soviet aircraft had yet flown, and though the prototype proved troublesome in flight tests, particularly with regard to its temperamental AL-7F engine, the performance it demonstrated showed excellent potential, and production had been authorized even before the aircraft had undergone its state trials.

Recycling a designation from an earlier Sukhoi piston engine fighter design that had never entered production, the aircraft became the Su-7, and after it was revealed during the air parade in Tushino in June 1956, the type became 'Fitter' to NATO (and then Fitter-A once other variants appeared).

Second prototype

A second prototype, the S-2, was produced that more closely resembled production aircraft, featuring a lengthened fuselage with greater fuel capacity and two Nudelman-Richter NR-30 30mm (1.18in) cannon in the wing roots, replacing the trio of such weapons carried by the S-1. The first production Su-7 was delivered in the spring of 1958, although the first 20 or so aircraft were used exclusively for trial work as the Su-7 suffered from many teething troubles.

During this period, a 'wasp-waisted' fuselage was adopted as the area rule was applied to the aircraft, the forward fuselage was slightly extended and a slightly more powerful Al-7F-1 engine was incorporated. Entering service in 1959, the Su-7 was initially utilized as an air superiority fighter.

As early as 1956, however, modification of the design into a fighter bomber had begun, and the decision to concentrate on the MiG-21 in the air-superiority role saw fewer than 200 Su-7A fighters produced.

Su-7B production model

The S-2 was reworked into the S-22 fighter-bomber prototype, flying in April 1959, and production of the fighter-bomber Su-7B swiftly followed. The first production Su-7Bs entered service in 1961, retaining the Fitter-A NATO reporting name, and 431 were

Su-7BMK

The rough field capability of the Fitter was improved in the BML and BMK variants, though the aircraft remained demanding on field length. This Su-7BMK was serving with the VVS in the Trans-Baikal Military District in 1978.

Sukhoi Su-7BMK

Weight (maximum take-off): 15,210kg (33,530lb)
Dimensions: Length 16.8m (55ft 1in), Wingspan 9.31m (30ft 7in), Height 4.99m (16ft 5in)
Powerplant: One Saturn AL-7F1-100 afterburning turbojet engine rated at 67.1 kN (15075lbf) dry, 98.1kN (22050lbf) with afterburner
Maximum speed: 2150km/h (1336mph)
Range: 1650km (1025 miles)
Ceiling: 17,600m (57,743ft)
Crew: 1
Armament: Two 30 mm (1.18in) Nudelman-Rikhter NR-30 cannon fixed forward firing in wings; up to 3300kg (7275lb) bombs or stores

ATTACK AIRCRAFT

produced by 1963. The need for greater range was recognized even before the Su-7B entered service and resulted in the Su-7BM, with increased internal tankage as well as wing pylons capable of carrying four 620L (136.4gal) drop tanks for ferry flights. Two hundred and ninety Su-7BMs were built before production switched to the Su-7BKL, with internal fuel capacity raised once more and with the ability to carry larger external fuel tanks.

A rough field undercarriage was fitted, which was also able to handle higher aircraft weights, and RATO gear could be fitted. This variant was also supplied in slightly downgraded form as the Su-7BMK for export, the aircraft proving a fairly successful product, with nine other air arms ordering examples.

Indo-Pakistan War

The biggest non-Soviet user was India, and the Su-7 displayed its robust construction during the 1971 Indo-Pakistan War, flying around 1500 sorties but losing none to enemy action, despite facing intense ground fire. On two occasions, Indian Su-7s were hit by Sidewinder missiles, and both times the damaged aircraft returned safely to base. Su-7s were also used in action by Egypt in 1967 and 1973.

Recognizing the potentially daunting nature of its high performance, the Su-7 was also built as a two-seat trainer, the Su-7U 'Moujik', which retained some combat capability as both cannon were still fitted, and two pylons (rather than four) were fitted under the wings.

The two-seater was also produced for export as the Su-7UMK. In total, 1862 Su-7s were built, of which 411 were two-seaters.

Sukhoi Su-17 and Sukhoi Su-22 'Fitter'

The Su-7 had proved fast but was demanding on runway length. The Su-17 added a variable geometry wing, greatly improving short-field performance and giving the basic Fitter design a new lease of life.

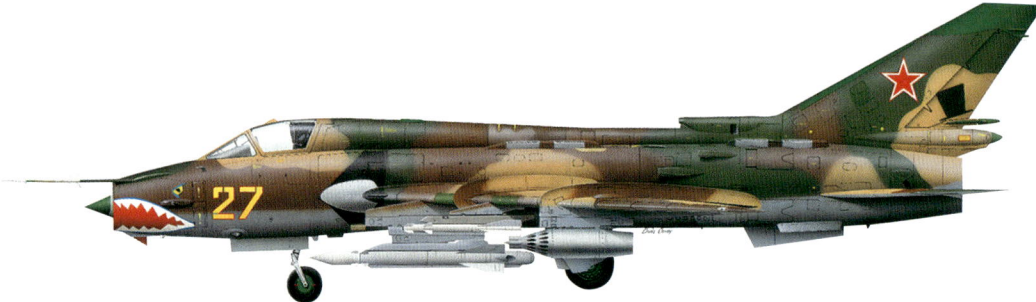

Su-17M-4

This aircraft was based at Templin in East Germany at the very end of the Cold War and was flown to Russia on 5 April 1994, by which time the USSR had collapsed and this aircraft became part of the Russian Air Force.

During the 1960s, the obvious vulnerability of long concrete runways to air attack became a concern to air arms across the world, and the Soviet Union was no exception. The ability to disperse combat aircraft, especially those operating in tactical roles, to small or unprepared airfields was seen as highly beneficial, yet the principal Soviet fighter bomber, the Su-7, was totally dependent on very long runways, and the addition of modifications such as RATO gear did little to improve matters.

As a result, Sukhoi developed variable geometry outer wing panels for the Fitter, and an Su-7BM was rebuilt as the S-22I to test the design. Flying on 2 August 1966, the S-22I was the first Soviet variable geometry jet. During tests, it was found that the jet's 'swing-wing' shortened the take-off run

ATTACK AIRCRAFT

by half and also improved the landing run. The aircraft also demonstrated a slight improvement in range, which, though still decidedly modest, was impressive considering the weight increase incurred by the wing sweep mechanism. Production was approved in November 1967 as the Su-17, and this initial version would be built until 1973, receiving the NATO reporting name of Fitter-C.

Su-17M

An engine change to the much more fuel-efficient Lyulka AL-21F resulted in the Su-17M, still referred to as Fitter-C by NATO, which also boasted increased fuel capacity, transforming the Su-17's range capability. When compared to the Su-7, the Su-17M could carry double the weight of weapons twice as far – all while retaining the Su-7's famed strength and excellent handling. The Su-17M was produced between 1972 and 1976, and 253 were built. An upgrade to the avionics systems resulted in the Su-17M2 (Fitter-D), built between 1974 and 1979, which could carry a much wider array of both air-to-air and air-to-ground stores.

During the same period, a two-seat training variant was developed, the Su-17UM (Fitter-G), since the aircraft had completely different landing and take-off characteristics to the Su-7. Produced between 1976 and 1981, the Fitter-G had an extended two-seater fuselage, which was subsequently modified back into a single-seater variant with the space provided for the second cockpit being given over to more fuel to become the Su-17M3 (Fitter-H) – 488 examples were built between 1976 and 1981. Further significant improvement to the avionics resulted in the Su-17M4 (Fitter-K), which flew in June 1980, and this variant would become the last Fitter to be produced when the final example rolled off the assembly line in 1990, by which time around 1000 Su-17s were in service with the VVS.

Soviet Su-17s saw action in Afghanistan, performing reconnaissance as well as undertaking ground attack duties as the primary Soviet tactical aircraft throughout the conflict.

Su-22

The Su-17 also found ready acceptance on the export market with the Su-20, a slightly downgraded Su-17M that was available from 1973. The later Su-22 featured a Tumansky R29BS-300 engine, which offered similar power to the AL-21F of the Su-17M but was much cheaper, although it was also larger and less fuel efficient. Produced in reconnaissance as well as regular fighter-bomber variants, the Su-22 was supplied to most Warsaw Pact nations as well as many other air arms around the world, from Peru to Vietnam. Iraq was the largest single non-Warsaw pact user, with most of their surviving fleet fleeing to Iran during the Gulf War, where they were eventually refurbished and pressed into service. Poland, the last European Fitter operator, retained the aircraft in service in 2024, along with a handful of Middle Eastern and Asian nations.

Sukhoi Su-17M-4

Weight (maximum take-off): 19,430kg (42,836lb)
Dimensions: Length 19.02m (62ft 5in), Wingspan 13.68m (44ft 11in) wings spread, 10.02m (33ft) wings swept, Height 5.12m (16ft 10in)
Powerplant: One Lyulka AL-21F-3 afterburning turbojet engine, rated at 76.4kN (17200lbf) dry, 109.8kN (24700lbf) with afterburner
Maximum speed: 1860km/h (1160mph)
Range: 1150km (710 miles)
Ceiling: 14,200m (46,600ft)
Crew: 1
Armament: Two 30mm (1.18in) Nudelman-Rikhter NR-30 cannon fixed forward firing in wings; up to 4,000kg (8,800lb) of bombs or stores

---

Su-17M-4
The Su-17M-4 was the final production version of the Fitter, this example was retained by the Zhukovski Engineering Academy but now forms part of the collection of the Central Air Force museum at Monino, Moscow.

ATTACK AIRCRAFT

Sukhoi Su-24 'Fencer'

The Su-24 weathered a complete change of configuration early in its development to emerge as one of the most successful combat aircraft of the 1970s. The Fencer remains a formidable strike asset.

Initial work on what would become the Su-24 began in the mid-1960s, with Sukhoi firstly pursuing a design based on the double-delta wing similar to that fitted to later Su-15s. This wing was mated to a fuselage featuring side-by-side seating for the crew of two and four Kolesov RD-36-35 lift jets in a bay behind the cockpit, arranged near-vertically to provide additional lift at take-off and landing and deliver STOL performance.

Designated the T6-1, the aircraft flew for the first time on 2 July 1967, but by this point, the liftjet concept was not viewed with as much enthusiasm due to the fact that apart from during take-off and landing the engines were dead weight occupying space that could be more usefully used for more stores or fuel.

In addition, in the turbulent air encountered at the low altitudes in which the aircraft was primarily expected to operate, the large delta wing delivered an uncomfortable ride to the crew as well as subjecting the airframe to unacceptable stress.

New wing

Drawing on work conducted by TsAGI, Sukhoi reworked the design to feature variable geometry wings instead, discarding the delta wing and liftjets but with the fuselage and tail remaining largely the same as before. Making its first flight on 17 January 1970, the modified prototype, now designated the T6-2I, delivered promising results. The first production aircraft appeared in December 1971, but early aircraft were used exclusively for trials and development work until the first VVS unit formed on the Su-24 in 1973, becoming operational two years later. Early aircraft were dubbed Fencer-A by NATO, and although improvements appeared in production Su-24s – leading them to be dubbed Fencer-B and Fencer-C in the West – all were simply designated 'Su-24' in the USSR.

Changes that appeared during the early production period included discarding the variable engine inlets, which had proved troublesome, in exchange for simpler fixed inlets, which though they limited speed to Mach 1.4

Above & opposite:

Today, most Su-24s are finished in a grey scheme but early examples such as this very heavily armed Fencer-C were painted in this green and brown over sky blue scheme befitting their tactical role.

Sukhoi Su-24
Weight (maximum take-off): 39,700kg (87,524lb)
Dimensions: Length 22.67m (74ft 5in), Wingspan 17.64m (57ft 10in) wings spread, 10.37m (34ft) wings swept, Height 5.92m (19ft 5in)
Powerplant: Two Saturn AL-21-FZ afterburning turbojet engines, each rated at 76.4kN (17175lbf) dry, 109.8kN (24675lbf) with afterburner
Maximum speed: 1700km/h (1056mph)
Range: 2775km (1724 miles)
Ceiling: 11,000m (36,090ft)
Crew: 2
Armament: One 23mm (0.91in) Gryazev-Shipunov GSh-6-23M rotary cannon fixed, forward firing in lower fuselage; up to 7000kg (15,432lb) bombs, missiles, or stores

ATTACK AIRCRAFT

were much less problematic in service. Higher speeds than this had been discovered to be largely impractical and unnecessary at low altitude anyway. In addition, a new fin with a distinctive kink was introduced, internal fuel capacity was increased by 1000L (220gal), a different aerofoil section was adopted for the wing, and targeting, countermeasures and other avionics were greatly improved.

Su-24M variant

In 1978 a substantially modified variant entered production, the Su-24M (Fencer-D). Although aircrew transitioning to the Su-24 were generally pleased with its performance and handling, its avionics and systems were complicated and unreliable. The Su-24M introduced an updated version of the nav-attack system, the PNS-24M Tiger, featuring the *Kayra-24M* (Grebe) laser designation system, which replaced the electro-optic targeting system previously carried. The PNS-24M also incorporated new IRS, radio altimeter, radio navigation, autopilot and central processor to deliver much-improved performance under operational conditions.

Countermeasures were improved with two sets of upward-firing chaff dispensers, and range performance was enhanced by the addition of a retractable refuelling probe ahead of the cockpit, resulting in an aircraft that could now realistically perform strategic missions as well as the tactical sorties it was previously restricted to. At broadly the same time as the Su-24M was being developed, Sukhoi was also working on a reconnaissance derivative of the Su-24, this emerging as the Su-24MR (Fencer-E), which flew in September 1980. Featuring an IR imager, TV camera under the forward fuselage, panoramic stills camera in the nose, oblique camera under the port main intake and an MR-1 side-looking airborne radar, the Su-24MR could carry a radiation monitoring pod on the starboard wing pylon, and SIGINT pod, or laser imaging scanner pod, under the fuselage. An electronic warfare version was developed concurrently to perform SIGINT and electronic countermeasures tasks, performing its first flight in December 1979, though fewer than 20 examples were built as the Su-24MP, which was assigned the reporting name Fencer-F and entered service in 1983.

Middle East service

When it was developed, the Fencer was not intended to be exported. However, during the 1980s, this restriction was eased, and an export standard Su-24MK was produced in the late 1980s featuring downgraded avionics in standard Soviet fashion. Syria, Libya, Algeria and Iraq all obtained Su-24s, and Iran became a Fencer user after the Iraqi Su-24s flew to Iran at the outset of the 1991 Gulf War, subsequently ordering a further 14 examples from Russia. In 2024, the Su-24 remains a significant component of Russian Aerospace Forces, with Ukraine operating a fleet of around 20 of the aircraft that they inherited when the Soviet Union broke up. Algeria, Iran, Syria and Sudan all maintain small fleets of Su-24s.

53

ATTACK AIRCRAFT

Mikoyan-Gurevich MiG-27 'Flogger'

During the early 1970s, the MiG-23 began to be developed as a dedicated fighter-bomber, eventually changing significantly enough to be redesignated the MiG-27, though it retained the Flogger reporting name.

The 1960s saw the Soviet Union fielding the MiG-17 and Su-7 as its primary fighter bombers, and by the latter part of the decade, the former aircraft was looking increasingly vulnerable due to its ageing design, whilst the Su-7 had serious payload and range limitations. A replacement fighter bomber was sought, and at the same time as Sukhoi developed their Su-17, Mikoyan OKB decided the most straightforward answer to the requirement was to develop a ground attack version of their MiG-23, which was then about to enter service.

The fourth prototype MiG-23 was modified into the MiG-23Sh – standing for *Shturmovik* ('Stormbird'), the traditional nickname given to Soviet ground-attack types since the iconic Ilyushin Il-2 of World War II – and submitted for trials.

Despite proving unsuitable for the role in its initial form, the MiG-23Sh was judged to possess enough potential to allow further development to proceed, leading to the first MiG-23B, with B standing for *Bombardirovshchik* ('bomber'), a more thoroughly worked prototype making its first flight in February 1971.

MiG-23

The MiG-23B was immediately distinguishable from its air-superiority brethren by dint of its radarless downward-sloped nose, which was adopted to improve forward visibility. The aircraft also used a completely different engine, the Lyulka AL-21F, and internal fuel capacity was increased over the standard MiG-23S with the addition of two new fuselage fuel tanks.

The aircraft was heavily armoured in vital areas, particularly around the cockpit, and although the landing gear was basically unchanged, it was somewhat stronger (to handle higher weights) and fitted with low-pressure tyres (for rough field operations). Ultimately, less than 30 of the initial MiG-23Bs (Flogger-F) were built, as both the Su-24 and Su-17 had priority for the AL-21F engine.

MiG responded by developing a variant with the Tumansky R-29B-300, which was less fuel-efficient but cheaper and less maintenance-intensive. In this form, the aircraft became the MiG-23BN (Flogger-H). Over 600 MiG-23BNs were built, all but 100 or so being exported to Warsaw Pact nations. Downgraded examples were also delivered elsewhere. The MiG-23BN was replaced on the production line by a more thoroughly ground-attack optimized variant, initially designated MiG-23BM but redesignated the MiG-27 by the time

---

Mikoyan-Gurevich MiG-27
Weight (maximum take-off): 20,423kg (45,020lb)
Dimensions: Length 17.04m (55ft 11in), Wingspan 13.97m (45ft 10in) wings spread, 7.78m (25ft 10in) wings fully-swept, Height 5m (16ft 5in)
Powerplant: One Tumansky R-29-B-300 afterburning turbojet rated at 78.5kN (17,600lbf) thrust dry, 112.8kN (25,400lbf) with afterburner
Maximum speed: 1810km/h (1125mph)
Range: 1800km (1120 miles)
Ceiling: 15,600m (51,180ft)
Crew: 1
Armament: One 30mm (1.18in) Gryazev-Shipunov GSh-6-30A rotary cannon; up to 4000kg (8800lb) bombs, missiles, or stores

---

MiG-23BN

This Czechoslovak MiG-23BN was based at Cáslav air base, east of Prague, in 1980. The MiG-23BN served with Czechoslovakia and then with the Czech Republic until 1994, when the ground attack MiG fleet was retired.

ATTACK AIRCRAFT

MiG-27
The baseline MiG-27 was known as the 'Flogger-D' to NATO and this example was part of the Soviet forces based in East Germany during 1978.

it entered service. The variable intake ramps were deleted, and although this restricted top speed to around Mach 1.7, this was not seen as particularly problematic for a low-level tactical aircraft, and the modification saved weight. The landing gear was strengthened again, and the stores pylons were upgraded to carry greater loads, while the GSh-23L 23mm (0.79in) cannon was swapped for a six-barrel GSh-6-30 30mm (1.18in) weapon, and avionics were upgraded.

MiG-27
The MiG-27 entered production in 1973, becoming the Flogger-D to NATO, and 360 were built by 1977. A further upgraded avionics suite resulted in the MiG-27K, referred to rather oddly by NATO as Flogger-J2. Flogger-J is the reporting name assigned to the later MiG-27M, a simplified and cheaper subvariant of the -23K. The MiG-23M was the only version to be built outside the Soviet Union when HAL of India constructed 165 MiG-23Ms between 1986 and 1996, becoming the last MiG-23s or MiG-27s to be built anywhere.

Service use of the MiG-27 continued until the end of the Soviet Union, but the aircraft was retired in Russia during the early 1990s on cost grounds, with the Air Force standardizing on the Su-24 and Su-25 in the attack role. Both the MiG-23BN and MiG-27 were widely exported, and the last operational examples, serving with the Kazakh Air Force, were withdrawn in 2023.

ATTACK AIRCRAFT

Sukhoi Su-25 'Frogfoot'

A subsonic, heavily armed and armoured twin-engine attack aircraft, the Su-25 *Grach* ('Rook') has proved highly successful in combat in a swathe of conflicts across the globe.

Despite enthusiastically producing dedicated ground attack aircraft during and just after World War II, the Soviet Union subsequently neglected this class of aircraft, relying instead, like Western air forces, on modified high-performance air-superiority fighters to perform this task. It took the American experience in Vietnam to demonstrate that slow-flying, heavily armed aircraft were of greater value in combat with ground forces in difficult conditions such as the jungle, leading directly to the US AX programme of 1967 that resulted in the production of the A-10. Mindful of these developments, interest in a 'Jet Sturmovik' grew in the USSR, and proposals for such an aircraft were invited in 1969.

'Bathtub' armour

Sukhoi's answer to the requirement was the T8, a relatively slow but agile aircraft capable of carrying 2500kg (5512lb) of stores and operating from rough airfields of only 120m (390ft). The pilot was to be housed in a protective 'bathtub' of armour. Initially constructed of steel, the bathtub was made of titanium in production aircraft. The prototype T8-1 flew on 22 February 1975, and despite flight trials proceeding well, development initially progressed slowly due to the priority afforded to the Su-24 and Su-27.

Nonetheless, production got underway in 1979, and in 1980, two of the prototypes were trialled operationally in Afghanistan and proved highly effective. Subsequently, the first VVS unit formed on the Su-25 in May 1981 and deployed to Afghanistan in July of the same year, thus beginning eight years of constant operational service against the mujahideen. Su-25s quickly proved their worth in combat, proving to be largely immune to gunfire from the ground but vulnerable to US-supplied Stinger missiles when these began to be used by insurgent forces; however, improvements to the aircraft's internal structure lessened this vulnerability somewhat.

By the time of the Soviet withdrawal in 1989, Su-25s had flown 60,000 sorties. Two years later, the USSR was dissolved, and various successor states inherited Su-25s, many of which

Su-25

One of the aircraft from the tenth production batch to be built, 'Red 09' is pictured in the scheme it wore when serving in Afghanistan. The Afghan conflict would prove highly influential to the aircraft's development.

Sukhoi Su-25

Weight (maximum take-off): 17,600kg (38,800lb)
Dimensions: Length 15.36m (50ft 5in), Wingspan 14.36m (47ft 1in), Height 4.8m (15ft 9in)
Powerplant: Two Tumansky R-195 turbojet engines, each rated at 44.18kN (9930lbf)
Maximum speed: 975km/h (606mph)
Range: 1850km (1150 miles)
Ceiling: 7000m (22,965ft)
Crew: 1
Armament: One 30mm (1.18mm) Gryazev-Shipunov GSh-30-2 Gast cannon; up to 4340kg (9568lb) bombs, missiles, gun pods or stores

ATTACK AIRCRAFT

Su-25
'29 Red' is depicted as it appeared when it was based at Tutow, East Germany in 1992 shortly before the withdrawal of Soviet/Russian forces from that country. It is armed with unguided rocket pods and conventional bombs on the outer pylons.

remain in service today. The Su-25 is popular with pilots due to its excellent handling and has proved reliable and comparatively economical to operate.

Variants

Although the majority of aircraft produced were standard Su-25s, a few variants were developed before the end of the Cold War, including 50 examples of the Su-25BM target towing aircraft. As well as carrying the target winch and associated equipment fitted to one of the regular stores pylons, the aircraft can carry parachute and rocket targets, and retains full combat capability if required.

A trainer variant was also produced, the Su-25UB, as although the Su-25 is a forgiving aircraft that is easy to fly, it was deemed prudent to be able to teach pilots the fundamentals of low-altitude close support.

ATTACK AIRCRAFT

Sukhoi Su-25TM
Weight (maximum take-off): 21,500kg (47,400lb)
Dimensions: Length 15.06m (49ft 5in), Wingspan 14.36m (47ft 1in), Height 5.2m (17ft 1in)
Powerplant: Two Tumansky R-195 turbojet engines, each rated at 44.18kN (9930lbf)
Maximum speed: 950km/h (590mph)
Range: 1050km (652 miles)
Ceiling: 7000m (22,965ft)
Crew: 1
Armament: One 30mm (1.18mm) Gryazev-Shipunov GSh-30-2 Gast cannon; up to 4400kg (9700lb) bombs, missiles, gun pods or stores

The two-seater flew in August 1985 and was assigned the reporting name Frogfoot-B, with the single-seater retrospectively becoming Frogfoot-A, and like its target-towing relative, it retained full combat capability.

The fine handling of the Frogfoot also saw it modified into a carrier trainer for the Soviet Navy; Sukhoi produced 10 examples of the Su-25UTG in the late 1980s. They were equipped with strengthened fuselage and arrestor hook for practising arrested landings aboard the carrier *Tiblisi* (later renamed *Admiral Kuznetsov*).

Su-25K & Su-25UBK
As with other Soviet combat aircraft, export variants were produced with simplified avionics and systems, export single and twin-seaters being designated Su-25K and Su-25UBK respectively. The first export customer was Czechoslovakia, which purchased 38, and other countries followed suit.

A more advanced Su-25T, specifically developed for the

Nose pitot
Like earlier Su-25s the Su-25TM has a pair of pitot tubes mounted just above the tip of the nose. The right-hand probe mounts antenna for the tactical navigation system.

Air-to-air missiles
This Su-25 is firing what appears to be an R-73 (AA-11 Archer) short-range infrared homing air-to-air missile.

Su-25TM
Fully armed with an array of missiles and weapons pods, 'Blue 10' was almost certainly the first to be built to Su-25TM standard and was used extensively for trials work based at the State Flight Test Centre in Akhtubinsk, Russia.

ATTACK AIRCRAFT

anti-armour role, had appeared with more fuel for better range and with numerous improvements to the avionics and weapon systems. However, the fall of the Soviet Union prevented this variant from entering full production.

Since 1992, remaining Su-25s have been subject to numerous upgrades, and the aircraft has been used in various conflicts, from interdicting drug-running aircraft in Peru to flying combat missions for both sides during the Russia–Ukraine War.

Tail
The Su-25TM retains the taller tail of the trainer version, necessary to compensate for the increased side area forward of the centre of gravity. An Irtysh ECM system is fitted in the cylindrical housing below the rudder.

Tailplane
The horizontal stabilizer has full span trailing edge elevators; at the same time the whole unit can be moved to preset positions to trim for different flight regimes.

BOMBERS

Although the Soviet Union fielded excellent tactical bombers from the beginning of the Cold War, long-range strategic bombing aircraft initially lagged behind those of the West. Improvements in anti-aircraft defences in the late 1950s resulted in a switch to intercontinental ballistic missiles (ICBMs) to maintain their nuclear deterrent and saw Soviet heavy bombers change roles to become carriers for stand-off guided missiles. The following aircraft are included in this chapter:

- Tupolev Tu-4 'Bull'
- Ilyushin Il-28 'Beagle'
- Tupolev Tu-14 'Bosun'
- Tupolev Tu-16 'Badger'
- Tupolev Tu-95 'Bear'
- Myasishchev M-4 and 3M 'Bison'
- Yakovlev Yak-28 'Brewer' and 'Firebar'
- Tupolev Tu-22 'Blinder'
- Tupolev Tu-22M 'Backfire'
- Tupolev Tu-160 'Blackjack'

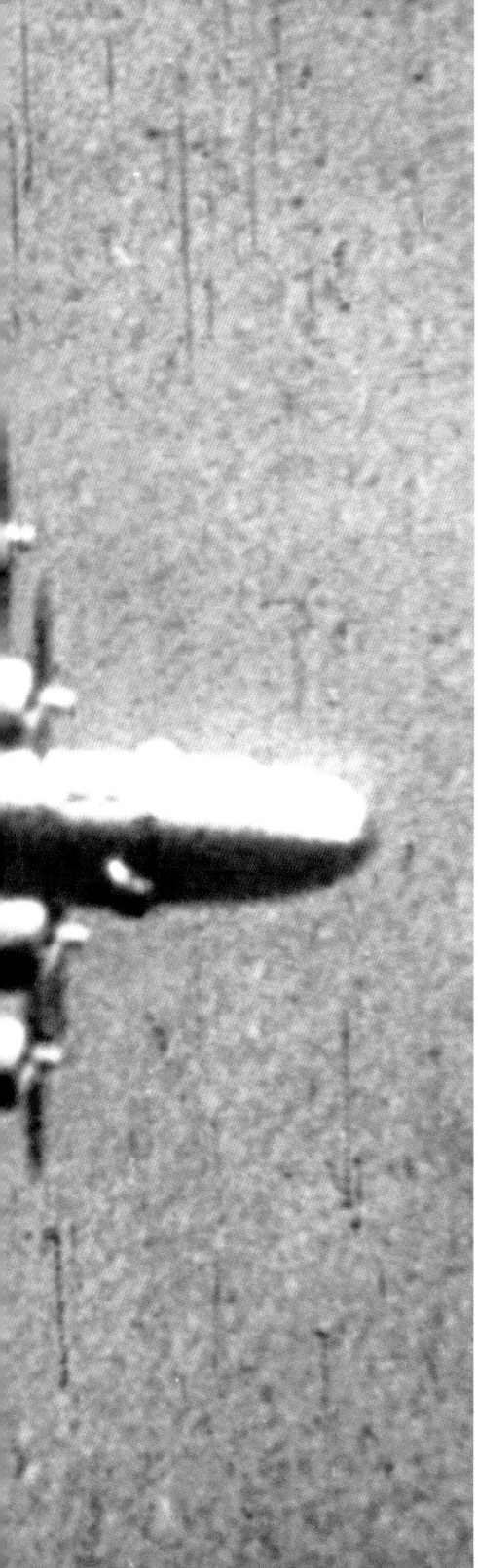

The Tu-4 ushered in the most psychologically tense period of the Cold War. Taken from a North Korean newsreel in 1950, an example of the blurred and scratched evidence that the Soviet Union had attained technological parity with Western strategic bombers and could potentially deliver a nuclear weapon on a wide swathe of targets.

BOMBERS

Tupolev Tu-4 'Bull'

A direct copy of the Boeing B-29 Superfortress, the Tu-4 filled an important gap in the Soviet inventory for over a decade and was the first aircraft to drop a Soviet nuclear weapon.

Although it fielded the impressive Pe-8 four engine bomber during World War II, this aircraft was made only in trivial numbers, and the Soviet Union lacked a credible strategic bomber fleet as the Cold War began. Seeking to redress this deficiency, Tupolev was ordered to reverse-engineer a copy of the B-29 as quickly as possible, four of which had crash-landed in Soviet territory after attacking Japanese targets.

Despite being ordered to produce as close a copy as possible, the Tu-4 differed in several respects, not least the substitution of metric standards, requiring different thicknesses of metal for the skin and structure, which resulted in a slightly heavier airframe. The engines were ASh-73s, a two-row development of the Wright R-1820 and unrelated to the R-3350s of the B-29 (though deriving from a common ancestor). Defensive armament was improved by the substitution of 23mm (0.9in) cannon, and both radio and IFF equipment were Soviet equivalents of US items.

Flown in May 1947, four Tu-4s publicly appeared at the Tushino Aviation Parade in August. This caused extreme consternation amongst USAF high command, as the USSR now had a bomber that could potentially reach US cities, a situation made all the more concerning after a Tu-4 successfully air-dropped the first mass-produced Soviet nuclear weapon, the RDS-3 atomic bomb, on 18 October 1951. As a result of the Tu-4's appearance, US and British fighter aircrew were thoroughly briefed on how to successfully engage the Tu-4 and participated in large scale exercises in which B-29s simulated their Soviet counterparts.

Over a three-year production life, 847 Tu-4s were built, and the aircraft were initially assigned to heavy bomber units, although the emergence of the Tu-16 and Tu-95 jet and turboprop bombers of greater performance saw the Tu-4 increasingly used on trials and transport work from the mid-1950s onwards. By 1960, the Tu-4 was used solely for transport or airborne laboratory purposes.

Several Tu-4s were supplied to China, beginning with 10 aircraft supplied as a gift by Stalin in 1953. Two further aircraft were acquired in 1960. The Chinese Tu-4s were operated for decades in China, and 11 of the aircraft were refitted with AI-20K turboprop engines between 1970 and 1973, continuing in service until the last was withdrawn in 1988.

A Tupolev Tu-4 on display in the Monino aeronautical museum, Moscow. The Tu-4 was as close a copy of the B-29 as it was possible to make. It is alleged that even manufacturing mistakes on the pattern aircraft, such as an incorrectly drilled hole in the left wing, was faithfully reproduced on all production examples.

Tupolev Tu-4 'Bull'

Weight (maximum take-off): 63,600kg (140,200lb)
Dimensions: Length 30.18m (99ft), Wingspan 43.05m (141ft 3in), Height 8.46m (27ft 9in)
Powerplant: Four 1790 kW (2400 hp) Shvetsov ASh-73TK 18-cylinder air-cooled radial piston engines
Maximum speed: 558km/h (347mph)
Range: 5400km (3400 miles)
Ceiling: 11,200m (36,700ft)
Crew: 11
Armament: Ten 23mm (0.91in) Nudelman-Suranov NS-23 cannon, mounted in pairs in each of the four remote control turrets and two in the manned tail position; up to 8000kg (17636lb) bombload

Ilyushin Il-28 'Beagle'

The first successful Soviet jet bomber, the Il-28, also proved successful in a variety of other roles. Simple, reliable and popular, the Il-28 was exported to over 20 nations.

Il-28
A reliable and relatively simple aircraft, the Il-28 was widely exported. Chinese examples like this one were initially supplied by the USSR but from 1965 China produced the aircraft as the Harbin H-5, operating the type until 2011.

Ilyushin OKB had flown the Soviet Union's first jet-powered bomber, the four-engined Il-22, in 1947, but the excessive fuel consumption of its Lyulka engines led to the aircraft's abandonment. The Il-28 was a smaller and simpler aircraft powered by a pair of RD-45s, unlicensed Rolls-Royce Nene copies, and the new aircraft flew almost exactly a year later on 8 July 1948. Only three crew members operated the Il-28: a single pilot, a navigator/bomb-aimer, who sat in the glazed nose of the aircraft, and a rear gunner housed in a power turret equipped with two Nudelman-Suranov NS-23 23mm (0.9in) cannon.

All three crew positions were pressurized, but only the pilot and navigator were provided with ejection seats, the gunner having to make do with a hatch in the floor if required to bail out. Testing of the new aircraft proved uneventful, the Il-28 demonstrating excellent handling and good performance, and it was ordered into production in May 1949. Over the course of the early 1950s, the Il-28 became the Soviet Union's standard tactical bomber, replacing the piston-powered Tu-2.

The adaptable Il-28 soon proved amenable to other roles. For example, a training version, the Il-28U ('Mascot'), was flown as early as March 1950 and was followed by a reconnaissance variant, Il-28R, in the following month, both of which were produced in considerable numbers. For naval use, the Il-28T was developed, able to accommodate two small torpedoes or a single larger one (including the RAT-52 rocket propelled torpedo) in a lengthened weapons bay. The Il-28 was also developed to carry atomic weapons as the Il-28N, with modified bomb bay and revised avionics.

Ilyushin Il-28 'Beagle'
Weight (maximum take-off): 21,200kg (467,38lb)
Dimensions: Length 17.65m (57ft 11in), Wingspan 21.45m (70ft 4in), Height 6.7m (22ft)
Powerplant: Two Klimov VK-1A centrifugal-flow turbojet engines, each rated at 26.5kN (6000lbf)
Maximum speed: 902km/h (560mph)
Range: 2180km (1350 miles)
Ceiling: 12,300m (40,400ft)
Crew: 3
Armament: Two 23mm (0.91in) Nudelman-Rikhter NR-23 cannon fixed forward firing in nose and two flexibly mounted in rear turret; 3000kg (6600lb) bombload

---

EXPORT SUCCESS

Given its excellent performance and comparative simplicity, it is unsurprising that the Il-28 was widely exported. The type was also built in large numbers in China as an unlicensed copy, the Harbin H-5, around 40 examples of which remained in service in 2024 with North Korea. The Il-28 would see combat with other air arms throughout the 1960s, even as the type was withdrawn from frontline roles in the Soviet Union towards the end of the 1950s. During the North Yemen Civil War of 1963, Il-28s attacked Royalist forces and bombed several Saudi cities. Egypt's Il-28s would also be used against Israeli forces during the Six Day War and the Yom Kippur War that followed. Further action followed in the hands of Nigeria in the Biafran conflict and with Soviet-backed Afghanistan against mujahedin insurgents in the early 1980s, the last known combat use of the Beagle.

BOMBERS

Tupolev Tu-14 'Bosun'

Despite proving inferior in trials to the Ilyushin Il-28, some 150 examples of the Tu-14 were produced and used by Soviet Naval Aviation for several years.

The Tu-14 derived from an interesting three-engined design, the Tupolev '73', that featured two Rolls-Royce Nenes under the wings and a Derwent in the rear fuselage. The improvement in thrust offered by the Klimov VK-1 development of the Nene, however, saw the design reworked to a more conventional twin engine aircraft – the '81'. Prototype construction began in the summer of 1949, and the first flight was undertaken on 13 October of the same year.

The aircraft's performance was inferior to that of the contemporary Il-28, particularly in rate of climb, and the Il-28 was lighter, easier to fly, and simpler to construct, but the Tu-14 did possess a better range than the Ilyushin aircraft. As a result, it was decided to put the aircraft into production for use as a torpedo bomber and aerial minelayer. A reconnaissance variant was also developed, the Tu-14R, but this did not enter production either, losing out to the Il-28R.

Entering naval service in 1952 as the Tu-14T, the aircraft received the NATO reporting name 'Bosun' and served with the Northern, Pacific and Black Sea Fleets. Production aircraft differed from the prototype in the arrangement of the nose glazing as well as providing the necessary torpedo crutches in the bomb bay, proving reliable in service and popular with crews. Withdrawn from frontline units in 1959, the aircraft continued to serve in secondary roles on test work and training flight crews. A small number of Tu-14s were reportedly supplied to China, but details of their service there remains obscure.

Tu-14

'10 Yellow' was the first serial production machine. The Tu-14 entered service just as other nations were abandoning the torpedo bomber concept and considerable skill was required to fly this fast jet at low level to allow successful torpedo launch.

Tupolev Tu-14 'Bosun'

Weight (maximum take-off): 25,350kg (55,887lb)
Dimensions: Length 1.95m (72ft), Wingspan 21.69m (71ft 2in), Height 5.69m (18ft 8in)
Powerplant: Two Klimov VK-1 centrifugal flow turbo-jet engines, each rated at 26.5kN (6000lbf)
Maximum speed: 800km/h (500mph)
Range: 2870km (1780 miles)
Ceiling: 11,300m (37,000ft)
Crew: 3
Armament: Two 23mm (0.91in) Nudelman-Rikhter NR-23 cannon fixed forward firing in nose and two flexibly mounted in rear turret; up to 3000kg (6600lb) of bombs, mines or torpedoes

Tu-14
Though it lost out to the hugely successful Il-28 and is extremely obscure today, the Tu-14 found its niche as a mine laying and torpedo aircraft, proving popular and reliable. '24 Red' served with the Soviet Northern Fleet in the early 1950s.

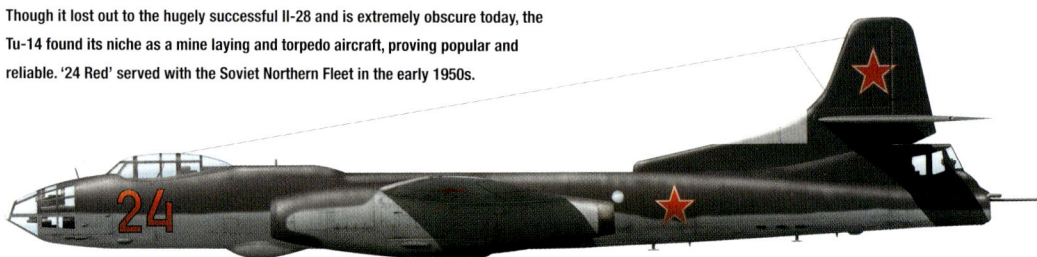

Tupolev Tu-16 'Badger'

Versatile, reliable, and rugged, though reputedly challenging to fly, the Tu-16 appeared in the early 1950s as the Soviet Union's first strategic jet bomber, though most of its service would be as a missile carrier.

Tu-16G
One of the more unusual Tu-16 variants was the demilitarised civil fast cargo Tu-16G, used for training Aeroflot crews as well as for delivering newspaper printing matrices from Moscow across the Soviet Union.

Entering service in 1954, Tupolev's swept wing Tu-16 won a competition against Ilyushin's enlarged Il-28 derivative, the straight wing Il-46, to become the Soviet Union's most important bomber of the late 1950s and 1960s. After making its maiden flight on 27 April 1952, the Tu-16 was found during state testing not to meet the range requirement specified, but the otherwise excellent general performance of the aircraft was sufficiently impressive that full-scale production was authorized in December.

The second prototype featured a lightened structure and increased fuel capacity and was broadly equivalent to the initial production standard. Service acceptance was granted in May 1954, the same month that nine Tu-16s took part in the annual parade in Moscow. Three months later, 40 Tu-16s took part in a flypast at Tushino.

Adaptable airframe
The initial Tu-16 Badger-A replaced the Tu-4 in the conventional bombing role, whilst the Tu-16A was adapted to carry nuclear weapons. The basic airframe proved amenable to modification, and several variants derived from the Badger-A were placed in service,

Tu-16K-10
Carrying a single huge K-10S anti-ship missile under the fuselage, the Tu-16K-10 was easily distinguishable from other variants by the prominent radar nose. 216 examples of this variant were built between 1958 and 1963.

Tupolev Tu-16K-10
Weight (maximum take-off): 79,000kg (174,165lb)
Dimensions: Length 34.8m (114ft 2in), Wingspan 33m (108ft 3in), Height 10.36m (34ft)
Powerplant: Two Mikulin AM-3 M-500 turbojet engines, each rated at 93.2kN (21000lbf)
Maximum speed: 992km/h (616mph)
Range: 7200km (4500 miles)
Ceiling: 12,800m (42,000ft)
Crew: 7
Armament: Six 23mm (0.91in) Afanasev Makarov AM-23 cannon, mounted in pairs in each of the two remote-controlled turrets and two in the manned tail position; up to 9000kg (19,842lb) bombload, usual load two K-10 air-to-surface cruise missiles

BOMBERS

including the Tu-16T maritime strike version, Tu-16N airborne refuelling tanker, Tu-16Ye for ELINT operations, the Tu-16G fast airmail carrier (also used for Aeroflot crew training) and the Tu-16S search-and-rescue aircraft which carried an airborne lifeboat.

Anti-shipping aircraft

Towards the end of the 1950s, attention switched increasingly to the use of the Tu-16 as a carrier for a variety of missiles and with an emphasis on naval operations, beginning with the AS-1 and KS-1 *Kometa* on the Tu-16KS, Badger-B, primarily intended for anti-shipping strikes. This was followed by the Tu-16K-10, Badger-C, which carried the large K-10S missile, usually fitted with a nuclear warhead. The Badger-D Tu-16RM-1 was derived from the Badger-C and intended primarily for the maritime reconnaissance role, though it retained the nose radar and could be employed to guide K-10S missiles launched from other aircraft.

The Tu-16R Badger-E was a dedicated reconnaissance and ELINT variant, as was the similar Tu-16RM-2 Badger-F, although the latter carried a greater amount of ELINT equipment externally. The Badger-G reporting name referred to both the Tu-16K and Tu-16KSR, which were rebuilt from earlier anti-shipping variants to carry various iterations of the large KSR missile. Later Soviet Tu-16 variants focused on the ELINT and stand-off electronic warfare roles.

Combat service

A total of 1507 Tu-16s were built, and like the Il-28 before it, the tough and adaptable Tu-16 saw ready acceptance on the export market. Like several other Soviet aircraft during this period, the Tu-16 would only experience combat in foreign hands. In the case of the Tu-16, both Egypt and Iraq utilized the aircraft in action, against Israel and Libya with Egypt and during the Iran–Iraq War and against Kurdish targets with Iraq. China was an early customer, and by 1956, it had acquired a licence to begin local production of the Tu-16 as the Xian H-6, over 200 of which have been built. Remarkably, China retained the Badger in production throughout the Cold War, and new H-6s were still being produced during the 2020s.

Tu-16 'Badger-C'
This aircraft flew with the 967th Long-Range Air Reconnaissance Regiment, part of the Northern Fleet based at Murmansk, in the late 1960s.

BOMBERS

Tupolev Tu-16

Weight (maximum take-off): 79,000kg (174,165lb)
Dimensions: Length 34.8m (114ft 2in), Wingspan 33m (108ft 3in), Height 10.36m (34ft)
Powerplant: Two Mikulin AM-3 M-500 turbojet engines, each rated at 93.2kN (21000lbf)
Maximum speed: 992km/h (616mph)
Range: 7200km (4500 miles)
Ceiling: 12,800m (42,000ft)
Crew: 7
Armament: Six 23mm (0.91in) Afanasev Makarov AM-23 cannon, mounted in pairs in each of the two remote control turrets and two in manned tail position, sometimes one fixed in nose; up to 9000kg (19,842lb) bombload

Tu-16 weapons load
The Tu-16's weapons bay is key to its versatility, enablying bulky payloads to be carried with ease. The voluminous bomb bay was originally designed for early atomic bombs.

Radar
Badger-C was the NATO codename for the Tu-16K-10 variant. This differed from preceding Tu-16 variants in being equipped with a radar nose containing the YeN 'Puff ball' radar set, credited with 180kW (240hp) peak power and a detection range of 480km (300 miles).

Air-to-surface missile
The Tu-95 'Badger-C' carried the K-10S missile, often fitted with a nuclear warhead.

BOMBERS

Tupolev Tu-95 'Bear'

An iconic symbol of the Cold War USSR, the Tu-95 has been continuously updated since it entered service in 1956. Its operational use has continued beyond the collapse of the Soviet Union, and it remains in operational service with the Russian Aerospace Forces.

Tu-95RTs
This Tu-95RTs was serving in the maritime reconnaissance role with the 867th Independent Guards Long Range Reconnaissance Aviation Regiment of Soviet Naval Aviation's Pacific Fleet Air Force at Khorol air base in 1968.

Responding to a 1951 request to develop an intercontinental bomber with an unrefuelled range of 8000km (5000 miles), Tupolev OKB concluded that the requirement could not at that time be met with turbojet propulsion, as the engines available were not sufficiently economical.

Unusual combination

Focussing instead on turboprop power, Tupolev developed a large aircraft with the unusual combination of swept wing and propeller propulsion. The NK-12 engines were developed from captured late-war Junkers turboprop work by a combined team of Soviet and incarcerated German engineers and remain the most powerful turboprops ever to have entered service.

The Tu-95 prototype flew on 12 November 1952, and series production began in 1955 and continued until 1969, by which time 173 aircraft had been built. Initial production Tu-95s (Bear-A) are easily identifiable by the absence of the prominent refuelling probe fitted to the nose of all other variants.

Weapons stores

As well as nuclear stores, the Tu-95 could carry up to 20 tonnes (22 tons) of conventional bombs, and bomb-aiming utilized a radar targeting system, with an optical sight available as back-up.

Optimized for the nuclear strike mission, the bomb bay featured heating and climate control for the nuclear stores, which required specific environmental conditions, and cockpit glazing with blast visors to protect the crew from nuclear flash.

Self-defence was provided by three gun positions, all containing a pair of 23mm (0.9in) cannon – two remotely controlled in the rear fuselage and a manned gun position in the tail.

One of the initial run of Bear-As was modified with an enlarged bomb bay to carry the huge 58-megaton *Vanya* hydrogen bomb, often referred to as the *Tsar Bomba,* to become the Tu-95V. This aircraft performed the only live air drop of this weapon, the most powerful bomb ever detonated in nuclear or aviation history, on 30 October 1961.

Tupolev Tu-95RTs
Weight (maximum take-off): 185,000kg (407,855lb)
Dimensions: Length 48.5m (159ft), Wingspan 50.04m (164ft 2in), Height 12.12m (39ft 9in)
Powerplant: Four Kuznetsov 11190kW (15000shp) NK-12MV turboprop engines
Maximum speed: 910km/h (562mph)
Range: 13,460km (8359 miles)
Ceiling: 10,300m (33,784ft)
Crew: 9
Armament: Six 23mm (0.91in) Afanasev Makarov AM-23 cannon, mounted in pairs in each of the two remote control turrets and two in manned tail position

BOMBERS

Missile carrier

Over the course of the 1950s, improved anti-aircraft defences saw the Tu-95 switch to the role of missile carrier rather than conventional freefall bomber. Initially, the large Kh-20 cruise missile was fitted semi-externally under the fuselage. To test the combination of Tu-95 and Kh-20, a series of drops of piloted MiG-19s were made from a suitably modified Tu-95 to investigate the mothership and missile interface and the behaviour of the aircraft at separation. Around 40 Tu-95K and 25 Tu-95KDs (all designated Bear-B by NATO) were equipped to carry the Kh-20 and remained operational until the late 1970s, but the prohibitively long time the missile required to be armed (initially 22 hours), its subsonic performance and its poor accuracy saw it replaced with the much more capable supersonic Kh-22. The latter missile struggled with development issues, however, and did not enter full service until 1987 with the Kh-22-armed Tu-95K-22, consisting of rebuilds of older airframes and known as Bear-G to NATO.

At the same time as this development was taking place, the Tu-95 was also being developed as a vital link in Soviet anti-ship defences.

The USSR had long been keen on anti-shipping missiles as a way to manage the overwhelming superiority in vessel numbers possessed by the US and NATO, and developed the potent ship- or submarine-launched P-6 missile. This weapon required guidance all the way to the target, and so the Tu-95RTS Bear-D was developed specifically to patrol and locate enemy shipping and then guide the missiles onto their targets. The system was declared operational in 1966, and Bear-Ds would be the type most frequently encountered by Western aircraft as they undertook their long maritime patrols. A strategic reconnaissance variant, the Tu-95RM Bear-E, was developed at much the same time, but only a handful were built.

Tu-142 derivative

Naval use of the Bear saw the emergence of a completely new line of development, the Tu-142 (see chapter 4). However, somewhat confusingly, late-production Tu-95s were themselves derived from the Tu-142 airframe. The Tu-95MS (Bear-H) revisited the missile carrier role and entered production in 1981. Carrying six of the low-flying Kh-55 cruise missiles, the Tu-95MS entered service in 1983. Initially carrying the *Osina* missile control system, the updated *Sprut* system compatible with the Kh-55SM began to be fitted from 1986. The Tu-95/Kh-55 combination remains in service today, with post-Soviet airframe upgrades allowing a greater number of missiles to be carried by each aircraft as well as much-improved avionics and systems. Curiously, despite its decades of service, the Tu-95 only saw its first active combat service in 2015 when aircraft began to deliver missile strikes against targets in Syria.

Tupolev Tu-95K

Weight (maximum take-off): 188,000kg (414,469lb)
Dimensions: Length 46.9m (153ft 3in), Wingspan 50.04m (164ft 2in), Height 12.12m (39ft 9in)
Powerplant: Four Kuznetsov 11190kW (15,000shp) NK-12M turboprop engines
Maximum speed: 860km/h (534mph)
Range: 12,500km (7770 miles)
Ceiling: 11,600m (38,048ft)
Crew: 9
Armament: Six 23mm (0.91in) Afanasev Makarov AM-23 cannon, mounted in pairs in each of the two remote control turrets and two in manned tail position; up to 10,700kg (23,590lb) bombload, primarily used to carry a single Kh-20 air-to-surface missile

---

Tu-95K
Frequently encountered around Guam during the mid 1980s, the Tu-95K was designed to carry a Kh-20 cruise missile (not fitted here), semi recessed in its belly, with the scanning antenna for its associated A-336Z guidance radar housed in a chin radome, although this aircraft is not armed with a Kh-20.

BOMBERS

Myasishchev M-4 and 3M 'Bison'

Despite being intended to strike targets in North America, the M-4 possessed insufficient range to fly to the USA and return. It did, however, serve with more success in other roles.

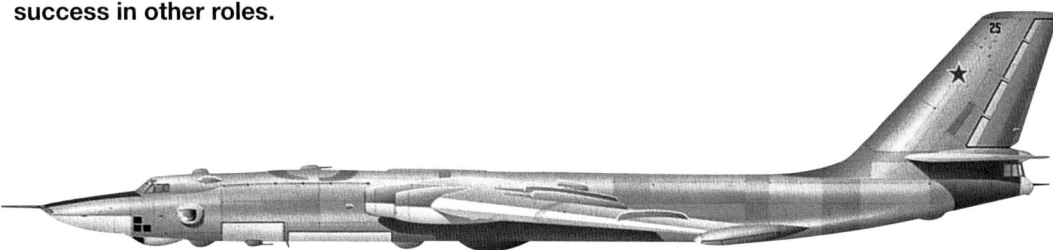

3MD
Unsuccessful in its designed role, the 3MD was a reworked version for the missile-carrier role, equipped with either the P-6, KSR or Kh-10 air to surface missiles and known to NATO as Bison-C. Only nine were built however, before the production line was closed in 1960.

Analysis of B-29 missions during the Korean War made it clear to Soviet planners that the piston engine bomber could not operate effectively when faced with modern jet fighters, and the advent of Western jet bombers such as the B-47 and Vickers Valiant prompted the development of a strategic long-range jet-powered bomber by Myasishchev OKB.

Bison-A

The resulting M-4 (dubbed Bison-A by NATO) flew on 20 January 1950, with production beginning in late 1954, and in the following year, 18 took part in a flypast – although as a hoax, 10 of these aircraft then flew past for a second time, leading US observers to estimate that 800 M-4s would be in service by 1960; in reality, only 34 Bison-As were ever built. This directly led to American fears of a 'bomber gap', prompting huge sums to be spent on building thousands of US bombers to close the perceived shortfall, which became arguably the most effective result of the M-4 programme. A weight reduction and aerodynamic improvement programme saw large changes to wing and airframe, the addition of inflight refuelling capability and the replacement of the AM-3A engines, with more fuel-efficient VD-7s leading to the redesignation of the newer aircraft as the 3M (Bison-B). The range, though improved, was still insufficient, but the greater speed and payload the M-4 offered over the Tu-95 made the aircraft attractive for the maritime patrol role, and the Bison served the Soviet Navy effectively in this role.

Bison-C

A few 3MDs (Bison-Cs) also built were able to carry two K-14S stand-off missiles. Both M-4s and 3Ms were converted to aerial tankers, serving until 1994 in the air-refuelling role. In addition, three 3M tankers were converted to become VM-T *Atlant* ('Atlas') freighters, with twin fins and large, distinctive dorsally mounted cargo pods for transporting oversize freight. These were mainly employed ferrying Energia rocket boosters to the Baikonur Cosmodrome.

Myasishchev 3MD
Weight (maximum take-off): 193,000kg (425,492lb)
Dimensions: Length 49.2m (161ft 5in), Wingspan 53.14m (174ft 4in), Height 14m (45ft 11in)
Powerplant: Four Dobrynin VD-7B turbojet engines, each rated at 93.16kN (20944lbf)
Maximum speed: 970km/h (603mph)
Range: 10,950km (6800 miles)
Ceiling: 12,000m (39,370ft)
Crew: 8
Armament: Six 23mm (0.91in) Afanasev Makarov AM-23 cannon, mounted in pairs in each of the two remote-controlled turrets and two in manned tail position; up to 18000kg (39700lb) bombs or missiles

Yakovlev Yak-28 'Brewer' and 'Firebar'

The successor to the Yak-25, the Yak-28 was intended primarily as a supersonic tactical bomber but proved sufficiently adaptable to serve as an interceptor, reconnaissance and electronic warfare aircraft.

Although Yakovlev OKB had already built a small evaluation batch of the Yak-26 bomber, developed from the Yak-25, this aircraft did not enter service due to various developmental problems, but it did serve as the basis for the development of the successful Yak-28. The availability of the promising new Tumansky R-11 afterburning turbojet led to Yakovlev rebuilding three of the pre-production Yak-26s into prototypes of a new tactical bomber, the most significant airframe change being to the wing, which now featured a more acute angle of sweep and was switched from a mid-mounted to a high-mounted position to allow clearance for the larger engines now fitted.

Although some doubts were entertained as to the potential of the Yak-28 – given the failure of the Yak-26 and distinctly modest success of the related Yak-27 – the new aircraft demonstrated excellent performance during testing following the initial flight on 5 March 1958. Approved for production as the Yak-28B, the aircraft was revealed at Tushino airshow in 1961 and was given the NATO reporting name Brewer-A. A precision bombing variant with the DBS-2S *Lotos* ('Lotus') datalink bombing system became the Yak-28L (Brewer-B) but proved unpopular due to its unreliability and its *Lotos* system's vulnerability to jamming. The Yak-28I (Brewer-C) featured improved radar and uprated engines, and as the Yak-28 was a fast and unforgiving aircraft, a conversion trainer was quickly developed, initially flying in 1962: the Yak-28U (Maestro).

Recon variant

In 1966, a reconnaissance variant, the Yak-28R (Brewer-D), entered service. This version saw the cannon deleted, but the Yak-28R retained the weapons bay of the bomber variant in order to carry photoflash flares. Three additional fuselage bays were provided and were able to carry three of the five different pallets of reconnaissance gear that were developed. Three of these were day camera pallets, one was a night reconnaissance camera pallet, and one was a SIGINT pallet. The Yak-28R

Yakovlev Yak-28PP

Introduced in 1970, the Yak-28PP was a significant combat aircraft for the USSR as it was the first Soviet electronic countermeasures (ECM) aircraft to enter service. The Yak-28PP was the last Yak-28 variant to remain in service.

Yakovlev Yak-28PP

Weight (maximum take-off): 17,470kg (38,515lb)
Dimensions: Length 20.34m (66ft 9in), Wingspan 11.64m (38ft 2in), Height 3.95m (13ft)
Powerplant: Two Tumansky R-11 afterburning turbojet engines, each rated at 46kN (10000 lbf) dry, 62kN (14,000lbf) with afterburner
Maximum speed: 1720km/h (1069mph)
Range: 1900km (1180 miles)
Ceiling: 14,600m (47,900ft)
Crew: 2
Armament: None

BOMBERS

also introduced some aerodynamic improvements as well as upgrades to crew comfort. This was the only Yak-28 variant to see active service, with reconnaissance missions flown over Chinese targets during border clashes in 1969 and later in Afghanistan. An electronic countermeasures variant, the Yak-28PP featured the cockpit and canopy of the Yak-28R, but the nose glazing of the Yak-28L was developed during the late 1960s.

It was designed to escort strike missions into hostile airspace and use its jammers and chaff rockets to protect the attack aircraft. This would be the longest serving variant, outliving its reconnaissance and bomber contemporaries and remaining operational until 1994.

Interceptor

Curiously, given that the Brewer was a bomber developed from the Yak-25 interceptor, the Yak-28 was then developed back into an interceptor again: the Yak-28P 'Firebar'. A tandem seating arrangement was adopted to replace the glazed nose position, which was now occupied by the *Oryel-D* ('Eagle-D') radar. Both crew were provided with flight controls, allowing the weapons system operator to relieve the pilot on long missions and also permitting the aircraft to act as its own conversion trainer. The bomb bay was replaced with fuel tanks, and two R-8M-1 air-to-air missiles were carried on the wing, where external fuel tanks could be fitted on the bomber and reconnaissance variants. Later, two smaller pylons were added outboard to carry a pair of K-13M1 missiles. Entering service in 1964, 435 Firebars were built in total, and the type became an important facet of the Soviet fighter force, serving until the late 1980s. None was ever used in combat.

Tupolev Tu-22 'Blinder'

Although fast and impressive, the Tu-22 suffered from a swathe of problems, not all of which were solved in service. Deeply unpopular with air and ground crew alike, the 'Blinder' nevertheless soldiered on beyond the dissolution of the Soviet Union.

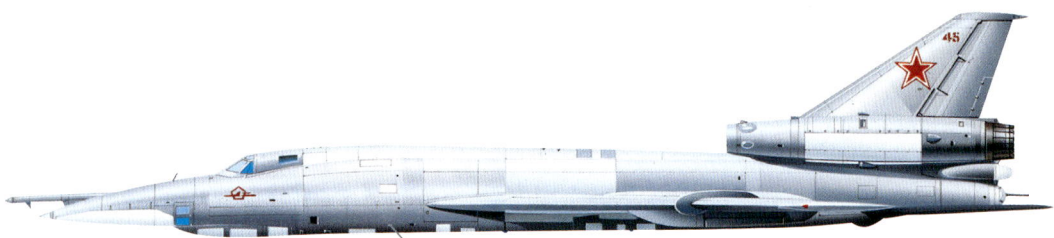

Intended as a supersonic bomber to replace the Tu-16, the Tu-22 utilised an unusual layout with both its engines mounted on either side of the vertical tail. This configuration was adopted to allow the wing to be as thin as possible and to avoid an undesirable tendency to pitch up at around Mach 1 that had been discovered in wind tunnel testing. It also proved beneficial in that it eliminated inlet losses and created minimal drag. The Tu-22 also dispensed with a co-pilot, not only

Tu-22PD

On the strength of the 121st Guards Sevastopol Red Banner Heavy Bomber Regiment, at Machulischi in Belarus, this Tu-22PD, a specialised ECM jamming variant, is depicted as it appeared just before its retirement in 1994.

allowing the cockpit to be narrower but proving attractive from a political point of view as it meant training fewer crew members. Flying for the first time on 7 September 1959, the aircraft entered service in 1962 but only 15 of the

Tupolev Tu-22PD

Weight (maximum take-off): 92,000kg (20,2285lb)
Dimensions: Length 41.6m (136ft 6in), Wingspan 23.17m (76ft), Height 10.13m (33ft 3in)
Powerplant: Two Dobrynin RD-7M each rated at 103kN (23150lbf) dry, 157 kN (35724lbf) with afterburner
Maximum speed: 1410km/h (876mph)
Range: 4900km (3045 miles)
Ceiling: 13,500m (44,291ft)
Crew: 3
Armament: One 23mm (0.91in) Nudelman-Rikhter flexibly mounted in remote controlled tail turret

original conventional bomber version, the Tu-22B, were built. Although fast, the aircraft was inferior to the Tu-16 in combat radius, weapon load, and serviceability as well as being extremely demanding to fly, and Khrushchev believed, probably correctly, that ICBMs were a more effective means to maintain a strategic nuclear deterrent. Even had this not been the case, the Tu-22Bs were subject to so many problems that they never entered regular service.

To salvage something from the Tu-22 programme, the aircraft was modified for the reconnaissance role as the Tu-22R, which retained bombing capability, and was known to NATO as 'Blinder-C'. 127 of the reconnaissance variants were built, becoming the most numerous versions. 76 of the missile-carrier Tu-22K ('Blinder-B') were also built, equipped to deliver the Kh-22 missile.

Limitations

In service the 'Blinder' gained an appalling reputation. Cockpit ergonomics were very bad and even were this not the case, the aircraft had extremely heavy controls and was difficult and tiring to fly. It is not a coincidence that 46 Tu-22U (Binder-D) trainers were built. Landing the Tu-22 was hard: the stalling speed was high at 290km/h (180mph), and the stall was sudden with little or no warning; the undercarriage was prone to bounce and was weak, and the aircraft was prone to pitch up on touchdown leading to a tailstrike. Visibility was poor from all three crew stations, with the pilot barely able to see the runway on crosswind landings. The wing design was not sufficiently strong and allowed aileron reversal to occur at high speed, a situation made worse by the fact that aerodynamic heating of the aircraft's skin at supersonic speeds could distort control rods, worsening the handling at all speeds.

The downward-firing ejection seats were especially detested because they effectively guaranteed that low-altitude accidents would be fatal; this was no laughing matter when one considers that of the 313 Tu-22s built, over 70 were lost in accidents. Ground crew also disliked the 'Blinder' with its high set engines being particularly difficult to service. Despite the problems, the aircraft remained in Russian service until the mid 1990s.

Amazingly, the Tu-22 was exported to both Libya and Iraq, both of which used it in action with some success. A solitary Libyan 'Blinder' delivered a remarkably precise bombing attack on N'Djamena airfield at supersonic speed in 1983, during the Chadian–Libyan conflict, and Iraq used the Tu-22 to destroy an Iranian fuel depot on the first day of the Iran–Iraq War, resulting in an Iranian fuel shortage during the war's early stages. Much later, Iraqi 'Blinders' were utilized to sink one supertanker and set another on fire during the so-called 'Tanker War' in 1988.

Tupolev Tu-22RDM
Weight (maximum take-off): 92,000kg (202,285lb)
Dimensions: Length 42.2m (138ft 6in), Wingspan 23.17m (76ft), Height 10.13m (33ft 3in)
Powerplant: Two Dobrynin RD-7M2 each rated at 107.9kN (24300lbf) dry, 161.9kN (36400lbf) with afterburner
Maximum speed: 1600km/h (994mph)
Range: 5650km (3511 miles)
Ceiling: 13,800m (45,276ft)
Crew: 3
Armament: None

Tu-22RDM

Also based in Belarus, this Tu-22RDM, Blinder C-2, was on the strength of the 1st Aviation Squadron of the 290th Guards Long Range Aviation Regiment during the mid 1980s. The Shompol SLAR of this reconaissance variant is mounted in the ventral canoe fairing.

BOMBERS

Tupolev Tu-22M 'Backfire'

The many flaws of the Tu-22 'Blinder' saw Tupolev come up with a more powerful aircraft with variable geometry wings. To conceal the fact that this was a completely new design, the aircraft shared the Tu-22 designation of its unfortunate predecessor.

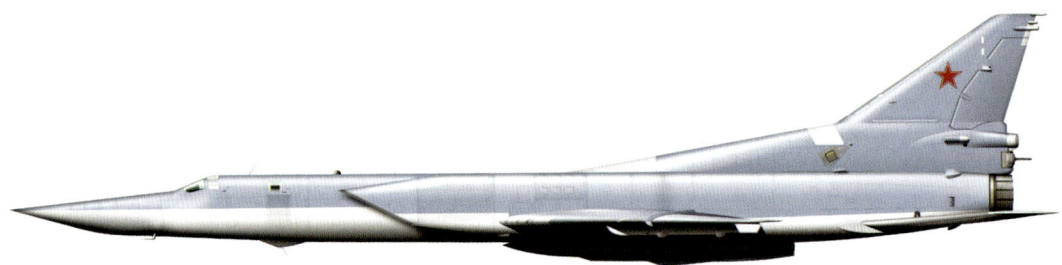

Tu-22M3
Typically anonymous Tu-22M3 as it appeared in the mid 1980s. Despite the design representing a great improvement over the Blinder, the Tu-22M was rushed into service. Manufacturing defects resulted in poor availability rates.

In the early 1960s, Sukhoi OKB came up with the T-4, a highly sophisticated bomber intended to cruise at 3200km/h (2000mph), whilst Tupolev promoted a less sophisticated alternative known as 'Aircraft 145'. Khruschev favoured the T-4, but after he was ousted from power in 1964, Aircraft 145 attracted more attention, mainly because it was much cheaper. Another reason was that China was seen as a more pressing threat than the US by this time, and the T-4 was regarded as an overly sophisticated aircraft to deal with China's less challenging air defences. Aircraft 145 was a far more cost-effective solution for dealing with the Chinese threat, and though the rival T-4 was built and flown, it never progressed beyond the prototype stage.

New design
The first of nine pre-production Tu-22Ms flew for the first time on 30 August 1969, and although the aircraft was officially an update of the Blinder, it was effectively a clean-sheet design, sharing only the missile weapon system, bomb-bay doors and a few other subassemblies with the earlier aircraft. The first production variant was ostensibly the Tu-22M1 (Backfire-A), but only nine of these were built, and all were used for development work (though seven of them were later taken into Soviet Naval service).

The first true production machines were the Tu-22M2, Backfire-B, of which 211 were constructed between 1972 and 1983. The M2 featured an area-ruled fuselage and increased span and was used both by the VVS and Soviet Naval Aviation. Capable of a maximum speed of Mach 1.65, the Tu-22M2 was usually armed with a pair of Kh-22 anti-ship missiles.

Speed upgrade
The first Tu-22M3, Backfire-C, flew during 1977 and was introduced into service in 1983. The new variant introduced new NK-25 engines, providing considerably more power but also allowing for a much longer time between overhauls. New inlets were fitted of the ramp type, and a thorough weight reduction programme saw some three tonnes (3.3 tons) removed from the empty weight of the aircraft. In addition, the maximum wing sweep was increased by five degrees. As a result of these changes, the M3 was capable of Mach 2.05, and range was increased by around a third. Armament was also improved with the introduction of the Kh-15 missile, of which six could be carried by the M3 on a rotary launcher in the bomb bay. Defensive armament was decreased, however, with one of the cannon in the rear turret deleted as part of the weight reduction effort. Two hundred and sixty-eight Tu-22M3s had been built when production ended in 1993.

In service – initially at least – aircrew were delighted with the Tu-22M, largely because it was not the 'Blinder' and was an order of magnitude easier to fly than the earlier machine. Handling was better, especially at take-off and landing, and the upward-firing ejection seats offered a much greater chance of survival than the downward-firing units of the Blinder.

However, poor quality control in manufacture and unimpressive systems reliability led to a poor serviceability rate. Most issues were dealt with by the M3 variant, and this has been subject to several major upgrades over its service life.

First combat

Combat use of the 'Backfire' began in late 1987 in operations in Afghanistan, but most of the aircraft's active service has been post-Soviet, with aircraft used in the conflicts in Chechnya, Georgia, Syria and in the invasion of Ukraine. Around 60 Tu-22Ms remained in service with the Russian Aerospace Forces in 2024.

Tu-22M3
Serving with Soviet Naval Aviation, '34 Red' is armed with a single Kh-22 long-range anti-ship cruise missile under the port wing. Alternatively up to ten Kh-15 air to ground missiles could be carried, six internally, and four on the wing pylons.

Tupolev Tu-22M3
Weight (maximum take-off): 126,000kg (277,782lb)
Dimensions: Length 42.46m (139ft 4in), Wingspan 34.28m (112ft 6in) spread and 23.3m (76ft) swept, Height 11.05m (36ft 3in)
Powerplant: Two Kuznetsov NK-25 afterburning turbofan engines, each rated at 145kN (33,000lbf) dry, 247.9 kN (55,700lbf) with afterburner
Maximum speed: 1997km/h (1241mph)
Range: 6800km (4200 miles)
Ceiling: 13,300m (43,600ft)
Crew: 4
Armament: One 23mm (0.91in) Gryazev-Shipunov GSh-23 cannon flexibly mounted in remotely controlled tail turret; up to 24,000kg (53,000lb) of bombs or missiles

BOMBERS

Tupolev Tu-160 'Blackjack'

One of the last aircraft designs developed in the Soviet Union, the Tu-160 remains in service to the present day. It is both the largest supersonic combat aircraft ever built and the largest variable-sweep wing aircraft ever built.

The Tu-160's origins lay in a 1967 requirement for a supersonic strategic bomber with a range of up to 18,000km (11,185 miles). By the early 1970s, Myasishchev's 'swing-wing' M-20 design was deemed to offer the most potential, but the project was passed to Tupolev due to its familiarity with large variable geometry aircraft. Development of such an ambitious and complicated aircraft was slow, although a mock-up was prepared in 1977, and the first prototype eventually flew on 18 December 1981.

Operational

A second prototype more closely representing the production standard only appeared in 1984, and the Tu-160 was finally declared operational in April 1987, operating primarily as a cruise missile carrier. It can carry six Kh-55 long-range weapons or up to 12 Kh-15 short range nuclear missiles – though conventional freefall bombs and other stores can also be carried. The aircraft was an impressive performer, larger and faster than the Rockwell B-1B it superficially resembles, and between 1989 and 1990, the Tu-160 set 44 world records.

Russia–Ukraine split

When the Soviet Union ceased to exist in December 1991, 32 operational Tu-160s had been built, with four more in assembly, all of which were eventually completed (the last as late as 2018). Most Soviet examples were stationed in Ukraine in 1991 and therefore became part of the nascent Ukrainian air force, but 11 of these were subsequently acquired by Russia.

Low-level Russian production was restarted in 2022, with 50 new-build aircraft on order as of 2024.

Syrian war action

The Tu-160 was used in action for the first time in November 2015, when several aircraft using Kh-101 cruise missiles air-launched over the Mediterranean carried out strikes in Idlib and Aleppo provinces in Syria.

Tu-160

This Tu-160, 'Red 24', served with the 184th Guards Heavy Bomber Aviation Regiment, subordinated to the 201st Heavy Bomber Aviation Division, based at Priluki Air Base (Chernigov Oblast, Northern Ukraine), c.1990.

Tupolev Tu-160 'Blackjack'
Weight (maximum take-off): 275,000kg (606,271lb)
Dimensions: Length 54.1m (177ft 6in), Wingspan: 55.7m (182ft 9in) wings spread, 35.6m (117ft) wings swept, Height: 13.1m (43ft)
Powerplant: Four Kuznetsov NK-32 afterburning turbofan engines, each rated at 137.3kN (30,900lbf) dry, 245kN (55,000lbf) with afterburner
Maximum speed: 2220km/h (1380mph)
Range: 12,300km (7600 miles)
Ceiling: 16,000m (52,000ft)
Crew: 4
Armament: Up to 45,000kg (99,208lb) of bombs or missiles

A Tupolev Tu-160 bomber during a combat training flight near the Engels air force base in the Saratov region, about 700km (450 miles) southeast of Moscow, 1990s.

RECONNAISSANCE, ELECTRONIC WARFARE AND UTILITY

In the form of the flying boat at sea and the biplane on land, the Soviet Union persisted, with some success, in developing aircraft configurations that had been largely abandoned by other nations during the Cold War period. As with other nations however, the USSR co-opted airliner designs for maritime patrol, electronic warfare, and other specialist roles. The following aircraft are included in this chapter:
- Antonov An-2 'Colt'
- Beriev Be-6 'Madge'
- Beriev Be-10 'Mallow'
- Yakovlev Yak-27 'Mangrove'
- Beriev Be-12 'Mail'
- Tupolev Tu-126 'Moss'
- Tupolev Tu-142 'Bear'
- Ilyushin Il-18, Il-20 and Il-22 'Coot' and Il-38 'May'
- Il-80 'Maxdome'

The Beriev Be-6 has been consigned to the plinth as its replacement, the turboprop Be-12, taxies past it in Murmansk Harbour. In some respects however, the Be-6 was superior to the later aircraft. The plinth mounted aircraft is still in place and was refurbished in 2022.

RECONNAISSANCE, ELECTRONIC WARFARE AND UTILITY

Antonov An-2 'Colt'

The ubiquitous An-2 apparently harked to a different age with its biplane layout but provided rugged STOL capability perfectly suited to the austere conditions prevalent across much of the Soviet Union.

When it flew for the first time on 31 August 1947, the An-2 appeared to be a total anachronism, but since then, over 18,000 examples of this slow but supremely capable utility aircraft have been produced. Around 5000 were built in the Soviet Union, followed by approximately 11,500 in Poland and 1100 or so in China.

STOL capability

Widely used by both military and civil operators, the aircraft entered service with the air arms of all the Warsaw Pact nations as well as many others, and although not originally intended as such, the An-2 has served as a combat aircraft on several occasions. First use under wartime conditions was during the Korean War, where the aircraft was employed to supply North Korean troops operating behind enemy lines. In Korea, the An-2's STOL capability proved invaluable; in normal conditions, take-off requires just 170m (560ft), and the landing run is a mere 215m (705ft). Flying low and slow at night over mountainous terrain, An-2s largely escaped radar detection, and as of 2024, the aircraft remains in the inventory of the North Korean Special Forces. The An-2 saw further use as a makeshift attack aircraft during the Vietnam War, during which conflict one aircraft was shot down in a unique air battle by a US serviceman firing an AK-47 from a Bell UH-1 helicopter.

More recently, the aircraft has been used in an offensive role in 1991 during the Croatian War of Independence and the Nagorno-Karabakh War of 2020, in which Azerbaijani An-2s were converted into unmanned reconnaissance drones. Since 2022, Russian An-2s have been operated in support of the invasion of Ukraine. The aircraft remains a popular type for several civil purposes, especially those which demand a decent payload capacity coupled with excellent slow-speed flying characteristics, such as skydiving.

An-2

The An-2 was found everywhere the Soviet Union or one of its client states maintained a presence. This civil example flew with Aeroflot's Arctic Directorate, seen here fitted with skis, these could be exchanged for wheels.

Antonov An-2 'Colt'
Weight (maximum take-off): 5500kg (12,125lb)
Dimensions: Length 12.4m (40ft 8in), Wingspan 18.2m (59ft 9in), Height 4.1m (13ft 5in)
Powerplant: One 750kW (1010hp) Shvetsov ASh-62IR 9-cylinder air-cooled radial piston engine
Maximum speed: 258km/h (160mph)
Range: 845km (525 miles)
Ceiling: 4500m (14,800ft)
Crew: 1 or 2
Armament: None; payload of 12 passengers or up to 2140kg (4718lb)

Beriev Be-6 'Madge'

Beriev's first postwar flying boat represented a huge advance over its wartime MBR-2 design, and the reliable and robust Be-6 remained in service for many years.

Designed immediately following the end of World War II and flying for the first time in July 1948, the Be-6 was a gull-winged aircraft with oval rudders reminiscent in overall design to the Martin PBM Mariner (though the Soviet aircraft was heavier and more powerful). Entering production in 1949, 123 would be built over the next eight years, and the aircraft was very widely employed in both military and civil roles. A tough and dependable aircraft, Be-6s served everywhere the Soviet Navy maintained a presence, from the particularly harsh conditions of the Arctic Ocean to the comparatively temperate environment of the Black Sea.

Maritime patrol

Initially used for maritime patrol and reconnaissance, Be-6 patrols would usually last around eight to ten hours, although some aircraft were fitted with extra tankage and could remain aloft for up to 20 hours. As the likelihood of the aircraft's survival against modern surface vessels and naval aircraft decreased during the 1950s, it was progressively developed into an anti-submarine platform carrying sonobuoys and MAD gear as well as thermal wake detection equipment.

Submarine tracker

Be-6s were used to detect and track submarines throughout the 1960s until they were replaced by the Be-12 and Il-38. The last frontline Be-6s in Soviet service were withdrawn in 1969, but the aircraft continued to be used for air sea rescue, transportation and fishery protection tasks until the late 1970s.

Approximately 20 Be-6s were supplied to China, and these were the last to remain in service. The inherent quality of the airframe was such that as the supply of Shvetsov radials dried up, the Chinese undertook to re-engine four aircraft with Wojiang WJ-6 turboprops as the Qing-6. The first conversion took place in 1970, and these aircraft continued to serve until the late 1990s.

Be-6

The Be-6 persisted in service for a long time. This Baltic Fleet example was photographed in 1973, the PSBN-M radar has been deployed and its retractable radome is visible below the hull.

Be-6 'Madge'

Weight (maximum take-off): 29,000kg (63,934lb)
Dimensions: Length 23.5m (77ft 1in), Wingspan 33m (108ft 3in), Height 7.64m (25ft 1in)
Powerplant: Two 1800kW (2400hp) Shvetsov ASh-73TK 18-cylinder air-cooled radial piston engines
Maximum speed: 414km/h (257mph)
Range: 4800km (3000 miles)
Ceiling: 6100m (20,000ft)
Crew: 8
Armament: One 23mm (0.91in) Nudelman-Rikhter NR-23 cannon flexibly mounted in nose turret, and two each in dorsal and tail turrets. Up to 2500kg (5510lb) of bombs, mines, torpedoes, or stores

RECONNAISSANCE, ELECTRONIC WARFARE AND UTILITY

Beriev Be-10 'Mallow'

The first turbojet-powered flying boat to enter service, the Be-10 set a number of class records but proved to be difficult to fly and somewhat accident prone. Fewer than 30 production aircraft were built, serving for less than a decade.

Development of Beriev's first jet-powered flying boat began in 1947 and resulted in the construction of the R.1, a straight-winged twin jet that suffered from serious hydrodynamic problems. Modifications to correct the issues took long enough that the R.1 was considered obsolete by the time they were solved, and attention moved to the Be-10, a larger and faster swept-wing flying boat promising higher speeds. First flight of the Be-10 was on 20 June 1956 at Gelendzhik on the Black Sea, following modification to allay potentially disastrous vibration in the rear fuselage. Performance did not meet the specification but was deemed good enough to warrant series production. Prototype testing was ongoing when production was authorized, and 27 aircraft were built between 1958 and 1961.

Be-10s replaced the Be-6 with the two squadrons of the 977th Independent Naval Long-range Reconnaissance Air Regiment, and these would become the only two units to operate the type. Despite the Be-10 setting 12 records, none of which have

Be-10
Delivering a huge leap in performance over the Be-6, the Be-10 remains one of very few jet-powered flying boats ever to enter service but developed an unfortunate reputation as unsafe.

ever been broken, accidents began to occur, with two production aircraft lost in acceptance and test flights crashes, one fatally. A third aircraft was lucky to survive when the cockpit glazing failed at altitude. Gases released by firing the nose guns caused compressor surges, and water was ingested into the engines on take-off and landing. The bugs were gradually worked out in service, but two more aircraft had been fatally lost by 1963, and there was a general mistrust of the aircraft amongst crews and little enthusiasm for the type at Naval Aviation Headquarters, resulting in the aircraft being little flown after 1964.

All Be-10s were withdrawn in 1968, having spent most of the previous four years in storage on dry land, an inauspicious end for this undeniably impressive aircraft.

Beriev Be-10 'Mallow'
Weight (maximum take-off): 48,500kg (106,924lb)
Dimensions: Length 31.45m (103ft 2in), Wingspan 28.6m (93ft 10in), Height 10.7m (35ft 1in)
Powerplant: Two Lyul'ka AL-7PB turbojets, each rated at 71.2kN (16,000lbf)
Maximum speed: 910km/h (570mph)
Range: 2895km (1799 miles)
Ceiling: 12,500m (41,000ft)
Crew: 3
Armament: Two 23mm (0.91in) Afanasev Makarov AM-23 cannon fixed forward firing on fuselage sides, and two in radar-controlled tail turret; up to 3000kg (6600lb) of bombs, mines, torpedoes or stores

Yakovlev Yak-27 'Mangrove'

Another example of Yakovlev's diverse family of supersonic twins, the Yak-27 reconnaissance aircraft represented an intermediate stage between the original Yak-25 interceptor and the more powerful Yak-28 bomber.

An offshoot of the Yak-26 bomber, which never entered serial production, the Yak-27 was initially schemed as an interceptor design. Two prototypes of this initial Yak-27 flew in 1956, leading to production of a small batch of evaluation aircraft. One Yak-27 was flown in 1957 with a Dushkin liquid-fuel booster rocket mounted in the tail and designated the Yak-27V. Although possessed of a spectacular rate of climb, it never progressed beyond the experimental stage. Taking part in the flypast at Tushino in 1956, the Yak-27 received the NATO designation Flashlight-C, but this version would never enter service.

Yak-27R

The design was reworked into the Yak-27R reconnaissance aircraft with ports for various camera fits in the fuselage behind the wing and revised nose glazing. In this form, the aircraft was approved for serial production and entered service with the VVS in 1960, appearing in public for the first time in the flypast at Tushino the following year and receiving the NATO name Mangrove. The Yak-27R retained the single-wheel nose gear and short wheelbase of the earlier Yak-25 but featured an improved and enlarged wing of greater span, with leading edge root extensions, a dog tooth extension on the outer wing and a single fence on each side.

A blunt-nosed slipper type external fuel tank could be fitted under each wing, but even with these in place, the Mangrove was unable to match the range of the Il-28 that it was intended to replace, though it flew much higher and faster. It was also acknowledged to be a demanding aircraft to fly.

Nonetheless, 165 production aircraft were built, and the Yak-27R remained in service until the early 1970s when it was replaced by reconnaissance variants of the Yak-28 and MiG-25.

Yak-27R

With only 165 built, the Yak-27 was never a commonplace aircraft. This example of the most produced variant, the Yak-27R, is preserved at the Central Aviation Museum at Monino, Russia.

Yakovlev Yak-27R 'Mangrove'
Weight (maximum take-off): 10,700kg (23,589lb)
Dimensions: Length 18.55m (60ft 10in), Wingspan 11.82m (38ft 9in), Height 4.05m (13ft 3in)
Powerplant: Two Tumansky RD-9F turbojet engines, each rated at 37.2kN (8400lbf)
Maximum speed: 1285km/h (798mph)
Range: 2380km (1480 miles)
Ceiling: 16,550m (54,300ft)
Crew: 2
Armament: One 23mm (0.91) Nudelman-Rikhter NR-23 cannon fixed, forward firing in starboard wing root

RECONNAISSANCE, ELECTRONIC WARFARE AND UTILITY

Beriev Be-12 'Mail'

Retaining the gull wing and twin tailfin layout of the Be-6, Beriev's turboprop Be-12 amphibian has remained in service for over sixty years.

Performing its maiden flight in October 1960, and first revealed to the public at the 1961 Soviet Aviation Day festivities at Tushino, the Be-12 began to replace the Be-6 in the anti-submarine role in 1964. Although the Be-12 could not match the earlier aircraft for its ability to land on rough seas, the performance offered by the turboprop Be-12 was considerably superior to the Be-6. Production took place between 1960 and 1973, and a total of 150 aircraft was built.

ASW platform

As an ASW platform, the Be-12 utilized an APM-60Ye (later APM-73S) MAD system with the MAD magnetometer housed in a prominent tailboom, and an *Initsiava-2B* (Initiative-2B) search radar in a nose thimble. Sonobuoys were carried in the weapons bay, and a mission computer system was fitted. Up to 3000kg (6600lb) of stores could be carried in the weapons bay behind the hull step, including homing torpedoes, depth charges and mines. Two stores pylons could also be fitted outboard of the engine for torpedoes or depth charges, though these appear to have been seldom fitted on operational

Be-12
The MAD boom is prominent on the tail of this typical Be-12. Despite its more modern design, the Be-12 possessed poorer seakeeping qualities than the Be-6.

aircraft. As the Be-12 entered service, thought was being given to using it as the basis of a search-and-rescue aircraft, and an early production aircraft was altered into the Be-14 to include additional doors and a pop-up searchlight, with the MAD boom deleted. A doctor and flight technician were to be carried, and the aircraft could carry 15 passengers. The Be-14 programme did not proceed due to budgetary constraints, but in the early 1970s, a less thoroughly modified SAR variant, the Be-12PS, which retained the MAD boom and could carry 13 passengers, entered production with 14 examples either built new or modified from standard Be-12 airframes.

Still in service

The Be-12 outlived the Soviet Union and remained in limited service in 2024, with nine on the strength of the Black Sea Fleet and a further two operational with Ukraine.

Beriev Be-12 'Mail'
Weight (maximum take-off): 36,000kg (79,366lb)
Dimensions: Length 30.11m (98ft 9in), Wingspan 29.84m (97ft 11in), Height 7.94m (26ft 1in)
Powerplant: Two 3964kW (5316hp) Ivchenko AI-20D turboprop engines
Maximum speed: 530km/h (330mph)
Range: 3300km (2100 miles)
Ceiling: 8000m (26,000ft)
Crew: 4
Armament: Up to 3000kg (6600lb) of torpedoes, mines, depth charges or stores

RECONNAISSANCE, ELECTRONIC WARFARE AND UTILITY

Tupolev Tu-126 'Moss'

Derived from the spectacular Tu-114 swept-wing turboprop airliner, the Tu-126 was the Soviet Union's first AWACS aircraft and was shrouded in secrecy for many years.

Mindful of the enormous expense required to build a ground-based radar detection network to warn of an attack across the Soviet Union's huge northern border, the Soviet Union decided instead to develop an airborne warning radar system. Initial efforts focused on the Tu-95 and its Tu-116 VIP transport derivative, but neither of these had a sufficiently capacious fuselage to house the equipment required. The Tu-114 airliner, itself featuring the wings and tail of the Tu-95, possessed a fuselage of greater volume, which solved earlier problems with fitting the crew of radar operators as well as cooling equipment for the electronic equipment aboard.

Flown in January 1962, tests revealed that the rotodome-mounted *Liana* radar performed better over water than land and that the efficiency of the system was compromised by the contra-rotating propellers, a problem improved but never entirely eradicated by the later installation of the *Shmel* ('Bumblebee') radar.

Tu-126

Very large, powerful and fast, the Tu-126 was an impressive aircraft let down somewhat by the performance of its electronic equipment. This example was photographed over the Mediterranean in 1972.

Nonetheless, performance of the *Liana* was considered acceptable for the detection of high-flying bombers, and the aircraft entered service during 1965. Once NATO aircraft switched to low-level incursions, the Tu-126 had to fly at low level too as the *Liana* could only illuminate targets from below. By 1970, Tu-126 patrols were being flown at around 600m (2000ft) – unusually low for such a large and high-speed aircraft.

In service, the Tu-126 was not popular with its crew of radar operators and technicians. Temperatures aboard the aircraft were high due to the large amount of electrical equipment aboard, and noise levels were also unpleasantly high. By contrast, the flight crew, seated well forward of the aircraft propellers, had a much more comfortable experience. However, the lack of shielding from the intense electromagnetic radiation of the *Liana* radar affected everyone aboard. This coupled with microwave equipment onboard led to health problems amongst crews. Despite these issues, the 13 Tu-126s built were kept in service until 1981, although at least one example was retained on experimental duties until the late 1980s.

Tupolev Tu-126 'Moss'
Weight (maximum take-off): 175,000kg (385,809lb)
Dimensions: Length 56.5m (185ft 4in), Wingspan 51.4m (168ft 8in), Height 16.05m (52ft 8in)
Powerplant: Four 11,033kW (14,795hp) Kuznetsov NK-12MV turboprop engines
Maximum speed: 790km/h (490mph)
Range: 7000km (4300 miles)
Ceiling: 10,700m (35,100ft)
Crew: 12 (a second complete crew was carried on operational missions)
Armament: None

RECONNAISSANCE, ELECTRONIC WARFARE AND UTILITY

Tupolev Tu-142 'Bear'

A dedicated maritime patrol derivative of the Tu-95, the Tu-142 matured into a highly capable ASW platform that remains in service in small numbers with Russian Aerospace Forces.

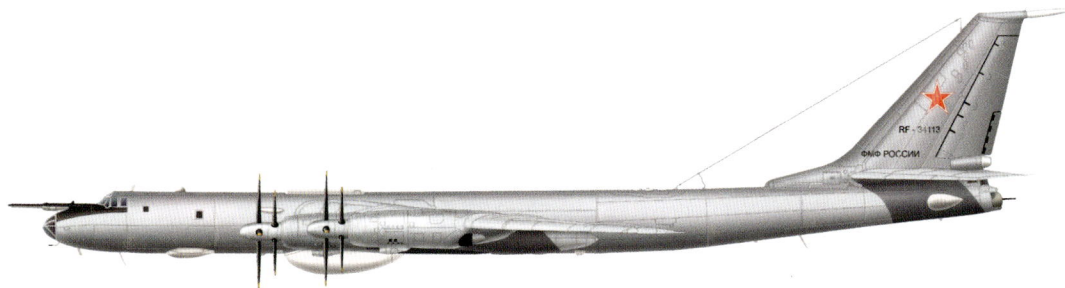

Work began on a naval Tu-95 derivative as early as 1963, but the first of three prototypes of the Tu-142 did not fly until 18 July 1968. The new aircraft differed from the Tu-95 most obviously in that its forward fuselage was stretched by 1.7m (5ft 7in), allowing a larger cockpit to be provided, improving crew comfort on long patrols and providing room for the aircraft's systems. The flight deck was also raised to improve visibility from the cockpit.

A rough field capability had been specified for the Tu-142, and accordingly the aircraft was fitted with three-axle, 12-wheel, main undercarriage bogies. The inboard engine nacelles had to be extended to accommodate such a large landing gear. The rough field requirement was abandoned soon after the launch of production, however, and only the first 12 aircraft were equipped with the 12-wheel undercarriage, with subsequent Tu-142s reverting to the standard four-wheel Tu-95 type. Other changes introduced on the Tu-142 included an extended chord wing, the deletion of the dorsal and ventral turrets and the use of the NK-12MV engines, which were nearly 30 per cent more powerful than the preceding NK-12M.

The combat systems of the Tu-142 centred around the *Berkut* ('Golden Eagle') search radar, originally developed for the Ilyushin Il-38, and complemented by an ELINT system, an infrared detection system and a sonobuoy receiver system. A weapons bay was positioned behind the radar fairing for carrying depth charges, homing torpedoes, mines or sonobuoys.

As production aircraft began to be received by Naval Aviation in 1970, Western intelligence believed the aircraft to be a variant of the Tu-95 rather than the new type it was considered to be by the Soviets. As such, the Tu-142 became known as the Bear-F to NATO. Early operations revealed several shortcomings with problematic handling and an unreliable avionics suite. The handling problems were largely eradicated through a major weight reduction programme. At the same time, the infrared scanner was deleted, and a simplified ECM system was fitted, which largely solved avionics issues. The ASW capability of the aircraft remained limited, however, and resulted in much development work, leading initially to the Tu-142M, which began to enter service in 1975.

Tu-142

The dedicated maritime variant of the Bear, the Tu-142 is easily mistaken for the Tu-95, especially as, confusingly some later Tu-95 variants are derived from the Tu-142 airframe. The MAD boom atop the tailfin is a useful identifying feature.

Tupolev Tu-142 'Bear'

Weight (maximum take-off): 185,000kg (407,855lb)
Dimensions: Length 49.5m (162ft 5in), Wingspan 51.1m (167ft), Height 12.12m (39ft 9in)
Powerplant: Four 11,033kW (14,795hp) Kuznetsov NK-12MV turboprop engines
Maximum speed: 825km/h (513mph)
Range: 12,550km (7800 miles)
Ceiling: 13,500m (44,291ft)
Crew: 10
Armament: Two 23mm (0.91in) Afanasev Makarov AM-23 cannon flexibly mounted in rear turret; up to 11,340kg of missiles, torpedoes, depth charges or stores, typically eight Kh-35 anti-ship missiles

RECONNAISSANCE, ELECTRONIC WARFARE AND UTILITY

'Blow' ESS
The effectiveness of the aircraft was much improved with the introduction of the *Udar* ('Blow') Explosive Sound System (ESS), which worked by dropping an explosive charge after a sonobuoy and using echolocation from the detonation to detect deep diving submarines. A new target acquisition system dubbed *Korshun-K* ('Kite-K') was installed. The system could detect surfaced and submerged submarines and communicate with other ASW aircraft and shore bases while also performing navigational tasks. Aircraft so-fitted became the Tu-142MK and also featured MAD gear for the first time. In turn, this was replaced by the Tu-142MZ, with the further *Korshun-KN-N* (Kite-KN-N) search-and-targeting system delivering a 50 per cent greater search radius. This variant, which also introduced more powerful NK-12MP engines, began its test programme in 1985 and proved formidable. The service entry of the Tu-142MZ only occurred after the end of the Cold War, with the first examples becoming operational in 1993.

One other variant was produced, a communications variant designated Tu-142MR (Bear-J), which was designed to undertake long-range communications duties with Soviet ballistic missile submarines, satellites, airborne and ground-based command posts in the event of nuclear war. The Bear-J replaced the Il-80 in the airborne command and control role.

Ilyushin Il-18, Il-20 and Il-22 'Coot' and Il-38 'May'

The Il-18 airliner proved the ideal aircraft to fulfil several tasks within the Soviet armed forces. Derivatives of the basic design served beyond the end of the Cold War and remain in Russian service today.

The Il-18 turboprop airliner flew for the first time in July 1957 and proved to be one of the more successful Soviet airliners. It was inevitable that the basic airframe would be pressed into military service, and the Il-18S variant of the airliner was used by the VVS as a VIP transport. Earlier airliner variants were converted into cargo aircraft for VVS use, and Aeroflot aircraft were often pressed into military service, seeing extensive service in Afghanistan, for

Ilyushin Il-20 DSR
Derived directly from the Il-18 airliner, the Il-20 did not require the wing to be moved forward as on the Il-38. The prominent fairings for ELINT equipment and ventral SLAR render this variant instantly identifiable.

example. However, the first of the Il-18 variants to be built specifically for military use was the Il-38 ASW aircraft. With the spacious fuselage and excellent range inherited from its

Ilyushin Il-20
Weight (maximum take-off): 64,000kg (141,096lb)
Dimensions: Length 35.9m (117ft 9in), Wingspan 37.42m (122ft 9in), Height 10.17m (33ft 4in)
Powerplant: Four 3169kW (4250hp) Ivchenko AI-20M turboprop engines
Maximum speed: 675km/h (419mph)
Range: 6200km (3900 miles)
Ceiling: 10,000m (33,000ft)
Crew: 13
Armament: None

87

airliner origin, there was plenty of room for combat systems and operators, and weapons bays were added in front of and behind the wings. The forward bay contained sonobuoys, and the rear one held standard stores for the ASW role, mines, homing torpedoes and depth charges, both conventional and nuclear.

A change in the centre of gravity of the aircraft resulted in the entire wing being moved forward approximately 3m (10ft), making the Il-38 readily distinguishable from the standard Il-18. It was also fitted with a prominent MAD boom protruding from the rear fuselage, and a bulbous radome for the *Berkut* ('Eagle') search and targeting system was mounted ventrally just behind the nosegear.

Entering service

Making its first flight in 1967, the Il-38 entered Soviet Naval Aviation service in 1969 and was assigned the NATO reporting name 'May'. 65 Il-38s were built, including a handful of a maritime search-and-rescue (MSAR) variant that carried a parachutable rescue pod semi-externally in the forward weapons bay. This pod was mistaken for a radome of some kind by contemporary Western observers. The Il-38s were popular with aircrew, proving reliable, possessing good handling and accruing an excellent safety record. Most served with the Soviet Union, but five were supplied to India, the last of which was retired in 2023. Russia, however, continues to operate the type, which has been significantly upgraded over the last five decades.

SIGINT variant

In addition to its maritime work, the Il-18 was used as the basis for the Il-20 signals intelligence (SIGINT) variant. A modified Il-18D, the Il-20 featured manifold antennas all over the fuselage as well as a prominent side-looking airborne radar (SLAR) pod under the fuselage and two fairings on the fuselage sides with ports for oblique long-range operation (LOROP) cameras. Entering service in 1970, 24 Il-20Ms were built, and the aircraft remains in service in much upgraded form with Russian Aerospace Forces, though the covert nature of its role means that the current equipment fit of the aircraft is unknown. A further development is the Il-22 airborne command post, which was given the NATO reporting name Coot-B after its service entry in 1970. The Il-22 is also liberally adorned with antennae, with the most obvious being a fairing on the top of the tailfin and a long ventral fairing running the majority of the length of the fuselage. Around 1980, a second batch of improved Il-22s were built, designated the Il-22M.

Around 35 Il-22s were built in total and were operated in Aeroflot markings to disguise their true purpose.

As of 2024, the Il-22 remains in service with Russia, currently in its Il-22PP form as an ECM platform, and one was shot down in early 2023 during the war in Ukraine.

Ilyushin Il-38

Weight (maximum take-off): 66,000kg (145,505lb)
Dimensions: Length 40.19m (131ft 10in), Wingspan 37.4m (122ft 8in), Height 10.17m (33ft 4in)
Powerplant: Four 3151kW (4225hp) Ivchencko AI-20M turboprop engines
Maximum speed: 645km/h (401mph)
Range: 7100km (4412 miles)
Ceiling: 11,000m (36,000ft)
Crew: 7–8
Armament: Up to 20,000lb (9000kg) of bombs, mines, torpedoes, depth charges, or other stores

---

Il-38

In Soviet service the Il-38 wore this overall grey scheme with only a small identifying number, in this case 05. There were very few windows provided for the equipment operators, just a few observation blisters for photographing vessels and aircraft.

RECONNAISSANCE, ELECTRONIC WARFARE AND UTILITY

Il-80 'Maxdome'

The Soviet Union's first widebody airliner, the Il-86 was modified into a flying command post as the Il-80 with a huge and prominent dorsal fairing above the forward fuselage.

The Il-86 flew for the first time in October 1977, flying its first scheduled service to Berlin on 3 July 1981 and receiving the NATO reporting name 'Camber'. Four examples were acquired by the VVS and modified into strategic airborne command posts intended to deliver nuclear command and control functions in the event of full-scale war. The first flight of the Il-80 took place in May 1985, but it was 1987 before the aircraft was fitted with all its equipment and systems.

'Maxdome'

During 1990, the Il-80 took part in exercises simulating the launch of ICBMs from the aircraft for the first time. NATO assigned it the somewhat bizarre reporting name of 'Maxdome', possibly as an allusion to its prominent dorsal fairing.

Painted in Aeroflot colours, although always operated by military personnel, the Il-80 possesses a comprehensive communication suite, including satellite communication antennas housed in the large dorsal fairing. Other fairings contain equipment for communicating with submerged submarines as well as with ground stations and other aircraft. The Il-80 is also hardened against the effects of nuclear detonations, is equipped with additional fuselage fuel tanks to increase endurance and features an inflight refuelling capability.

Constant service

The Il-80 has remained in service constantly since its appearance in 1987, and although its equipment remains classified, it has evidently been subject to various upgrades as various new antennae and fairings have appeared on the aircraft from time to time. Of the four aircraft originally built, three remained operational in 2024.

Ilyushin Il-80 'Maxdome'
Weight (maximum take-off): 215,000kg (474,000lb)
Dimensions: Length 48.06m (157ft 8in), Wingspan 59.54m (195ft 4in), Height 15.8m (51ft 10in)
Powerplant: Four Kuznetsov NK-86 turbofan engines each rated at 127.5kN (28665lbf)
Maximum speed: 970km/h (603mph)
Range: 3600km (2237 miles)
Ceiling: 11,000m (36,090ft)
Crew: Flight crew of 5, unknown number of technical crew
Armament: None

Il-80

Instantly recognisable by way of the massive canoe fairing atop the fuselage, the Il-80 has remained in service since the late 1980s. Despite the Aeroflot markings, this is very much a military aircraft.

TRANSPORT

The Soviet Union became justifiably famous for the sheer size of its largest transport aircraft and twice included the then-largest landplane amongst their operational fleet in the form of the An-22 and An-124. Of course many more modestly sized transport types were produced in the USSR, the An-12 is essentially the Eastern Bloc's C-130 Hercules and the VVS could call on a variety of tactical STOL transports. The following aircraft are included in this chapter:

- Yakovlev Yak-14 'Crow'
- Antonov An-8 'Camp'
- Antonov An-12 'Cub'
- Antonov An-24 'Coke' and An-30 'Clank'
- Antonov An-26 'Curl' and An-32 'Cline'
- Antonov An-22 'Cock'
- Ilyushin Il-76 'Candid', Il-78 'Midas' and A-50 'Mainstay'
- Antonov An-124 'Condor'
- Antonov An-72 and An-74 'Coaler'

An Antonov An-22 prototype military transport aircraft, July 1965. It made its international debut at the Paris Air Show the previous month.

TRANSPORT

Yakovlev Yak-14 'Crow'

Just as other nations were discarding the assault glider as a viable weapon of war, the Soviet Union developed their largest and most capable transport glider, the Yak-14.

During World War II, the Soviet Union had used gliders to great effect to supply partisans and other troops fighting deep behind enemy lines, but none of the designs available were capable of carrying vehicles, light tanks or all but the smallest artillery pieces. This deficiency was remedied with the Yak-14, capable of carrying a payload of 3500kg (7700lb) – more than enough to transport a field gun and tractor, or up to 35 fully-equipped troops.

Flying for the first time in June 1948, the Yak-14 was a simple aircraft built largely of steel tube with a fabric skin. A rectangular section fuselage was adopted to maximize available space, and both nose and tail could be swung open to aid loading and unloading. Additionally, the fixed tricycle undercarriage could 'kneel', lowering the fuselage and further simplifying unloading. Able to handle bulkier loads than any other contemporary Soviet transport, the Yak-14 saw considerable service throughout the 1950s, and 413 examples were built. In 1950, the Yak-14 garnered some fame as the first (and, to date, only) glider to fly to the North Pole, and the type's capability was demonstrated in March 1954, when four Yak-14s made a long-distance delivery flight, with supplies – including a large bulldozer – to a research station on an ice floe in the Arctic Ocean.

Despite such successful use, the advent of better and larger transport aircraft in the late 1950s spelled the end for the cargo glider concept, and the Yak-14 had disappeared from use by 1960.

Yak-14
Despite being a semi-disposable aircraft, the Yak-14 offered a load capability not available with conventional transports and was quite intensively employed long after other nations had consigned the transport glider to history.

Yakovlev Yak-14 'Crow'
Weight (maximum take-off): 6750kg (14,881lb)
Dimensions: Length 18.44m (60ft 6in), Wingspan 26.17m (85ft 10in), Height 7.2m (23ft 7in)
Maximum speed: 300km/h (190mph)
Crew: 2
Maximum payload: 3500kg (7700lb)

Antonov An-8 'Camp'

The An-8 overcame some serious early teething troubles to become a useful tactical transport, with some individual aircraft operating for several decades.

Work began at Antonov OKB on an assault transport late in 1951 known as the DT-5/8 to be powered by two Kuznetsov TV-2 turboprops delivering 4660kW (6250hp) each at takeoff, but it was not until 1953 that approval was given to proceed with prototype construction. The new aircraft was a departure from anything yet attempted in the Soviet Union; turboprop engine design was in its infancy, and the airframe broke new ground for the domestic industry, with its large rear door and integrated ramp allowing vehicles to be driven directly into the hold.

On 11 February 1956, the prototype made its first flight, but in testing it ran into immediate problems. The aircraft demonstrated a litany of severe handling problems, and the TV-2 engines were proving unreliable and possessed a short service life, with turbine blades failing after only 5–10 hours. Such was the urgency with which the An-8 programme was viewed, however, that the Soviet Council of Ministers ordered the elimination of the aircraft's faults.

First flight

Duly modified and fitted with Ivchenko AI-20 engines, the An-8 was deemed acceptable, and the first production aircraft flew in late 1958. Despite the improvements, the An-8's introduction did not proceed smoothly, and five aircraft were lost during the first three years of service. Further development work improved matters, and the An-8 was heavily employed in frontline units, with the type's most high-level operation occurring in 1968 when two An-8s were used by special forces to seize Plzeň airport during the invasion of Czechoslovakia.

Mostly withdrawn from military service by the mid-1970s, the An-8 enjoyed a secondary career in civil hands, initially with Aeroflot, with many examples subsequently being sold to overseas operators in the Middle East and Africa until the last survivors were retired in 2010.

An-8
Although it matured into an acceptable aircraft, the availability of the superior An-12 resulted in only 151 production An-8s being built.

Antonov An-8 'Camp'
Weight (maximum take-off): 40,000kg (88,185lb)
Dimensions: Length 26m (85ft 4in), Wingspan 30m (98ft 5in), Height 9.7m (31ft 10in)
Powerplant: Two 3,860kW (5180hp) Ivchenko AI-20D turboprop engines
Maximum speed: 610km/h (380mph)
Range: 2780km (1730 miles)
Ceiling: 9600m (31,500ft)
Crew: 6
Armament: Two 23mm (0.91in) Afanasev Makarov AM-23 cannon flexibly mounted in rear turret
Maximum payload: 11,000kg (24,000lb)

TRANSPORT

Antonov An-12 'Cub'

The An-12 proved to be a highly successful tactical transport and served as the Soviet Union's primary medium-range paratroop and cargo transport for over 30 years.

Antonov An-12 'Cub'
Weight (maximum take-off): 61,000kg (13,4482lb)
Dimensions: Length 33.1m (108ft 7in), Wingspan 38m (124ft 8in), Height 10.53m (34ft 7in)
Powerplant: Four 3125kW (4250hp) Ivchenko AI-20K turboprop engines
Maximum speed: 777km/h (483mph)
Range: 5700km (3500 miles)
Ceiling: 10,200m (33,500ft)
Crew: 5
Armament: Two 23mm (0.91in) Nudelman-Rikhter NR-23 cannon flexibly mounted in rear turret
Maximum payload: 20,000kg (44,000lb)

Antonov OKB developed a larger, four-engined civil transport from the twin-engine An-8 as the An-10 ('Cab'), which enjoyed modest success in Aeroflot service, although only 104 were built. The An-12 military derivative was an order of magnitude more successful, with 1250 built in the USSR, and production in China continued into the 2020s. Basically identical to the An-10 from the wings forward, the An-12 featured a large rear cargo loading door and a manned tail turret with two 23mm

An-12
Widely regarded as the Soviet equivalent to the US C-130 Hercules, the An-12 features similar performance and dimensions and has remained in service for decades.

(0.79in) AM-23 cannon. Initially flown on 16 December 1957, at which point serial production had already begun in Irkutsk, the An-12 became operational with the VVS in 1959. The aircraft was subject to only relatively minor changes in its production life, demonstrating the soundness of the basic design, starting with the An-12A, which began to be built in 1961 and which featured uprated AI-20K engines, a further four fuel tanks in the wings and updated electronics.

The following year, the An-12B entered production and was now powered by AI-20M engines that were more reliable than the AI-20K whilst delivering the same power output. More fuel tanks were fitted in the outer wings, and there were some improvements to internal systems, but the aircraft remained largely unchanged. From the

Rear turret
Unlike equivalent Western aircraft, Soviet transports were standardly armed, in the An-12's case with a pair of Nudelman-Richter 23mm (0.9in) cannon, as also used in tail turrets of the Il-28, Tu-14, Tu-16 and Tu-95.

outset, there had been calls to improve the range of the An-12, and additional fuel tanks were retrofitted to An-12s under the cargo bay floor. Aircraft altered in this way were designated An-12P or An-12AP depending on the variant that was modified, but similarly equipped An-12BPs were new build airframes and were also equipped with updated avionics. After 1966, production was of the An-12BK, which again featured improved avionics and cargo handling equipment, and this variant was built until the end of serial production in 1972. Civil An-12s were also produced from 1964, with the rear turret replaced by a fairing and military equipment removed. These aircraft would later be joined by various ex-military aircraft as they were retired from operational service, though many remain in service with Russian Aerospace Forces in the 2020s.

Service

In service, the sturdy An-12 proved to be an important component of Soviet airborne capability, seeing action in the 1968 invasion of Czechoslovakia and serving throughout the conflict in Afghanistan, where its ability to operate from short runways in 'hot and high' conditions on primitive airstrips that were unable to be used by larger Il-76s proved invaluable. Oddly, although the An-12 saw widespread service across the globe, only two Warsaw Pact nations, Poland and Czechoslovakia, obtained two aircraft each before the end of the Cold War. The first and largest non-Soviet user was India, which operated a fleet of around 50 aircraft from 1961. China obtained a handful of An-12s in the early 1960s and was intending to set up licence production, but deteriorating Sino-Soviet relations resulted in the production of an unlicensed copy instead, the Shaaxi Y-8, which flew for the first time in December 1974 and has been in production ever since. Easily identified by its longer and more pointed nose glazing, over 150 Y-8s had been constructed by 2024. Both these and Soviet-built An-12s remain in service with dozens of civil and military operators around the world.

An-12BP

Built in 1967, CCCP-11875 was operating in the ELINT role when it was lost in a landing accident at Ho Chi Minh City airport, Vietnam, on 8 July 1989. Like many Soviet transports it carries the civil Aeroflot livery and registration despite being a military aircraft.

Engines
The An-12 was powered by the Ivchenko AI-20, a turboprop engine initially troubled by very poor reliability and requiring a time between overhauls of merely 600 to750 hours. Development saw this raised to 8000 hours in the AI-20D series 5M engine.

Rear cargo door
Unlike the C-130 Hercules, the An-12's hold is neither pressurised nor air conditioned. Furthermore, the aircraft is not fitted with an integral rear ramp, the large rear doors swing upwards and inwards to provide access to the hold.

TRANSPORT

Antonov An-24 'Coke' and An-30 'Clank'

A successful short haul turboprop airliner, the An-24 was used by the VVS as a tactical transport and for other specialized roles. The basic design was modified into the An-30 aerial survey aircraft.

The An-24 flew for the first time in October 1959 and flew its first scheduled flight with Aeroflot in 1963. Production of a military transport variant had been considered from the earliest days of the programme, but the initial An-24T tactical transport variant of 1962 was rejected. Antonov reworked the design with a cargo hatch in the belly of the aircraft, extra fuel tanks, uprated engines and cargo handling equipment, and in this form, the An-24T was accepted for production and service. The belly hatch was never the best solution for cargo loading but was considered acceptable, and as an alternative to cargo the aircraft could carry up to 42 paratroops on folding seats.

VIP transport

An-24s were also used for VIP transport as the An-24S, a SAR aircraft, the An-24PRT, the AN-24RR for 'radiation reconnaissance' – fitted with air sampling pods to monitor fallout in the event of nuclear attack – the An-24RT

An-24T

Many Soviet military transport aircraft were finished in this smart pseudo-civil colour scheme. Now retired, An-24T '01 Red' forms part of the Museum of Long Range Aviation at Engels Airbase, Saratov, Russia.

communications relay platform and the An-24ShT airborne command post for the Red Army. Later-production An-24s, designated the An-24RT, were fitted with a small jet engine that functioned as both the APU and as a booster during take-off in 'hot and high' conditions.

AN-30

A heavily modified specialized mapping variant of the An-24 was also built as the An-30, which entered production in 1971 for both civil and military users. The most obvious change was the heavily glazed nose, referred to as the 'veranda' by crews, with optical sights and a raised cockpit. Various combinations of conventional and infrared cameras could be carried,

Antonov An-24T

Weight (maximum take-off): 22,500kg (49,604lb)
Dimensions: Length 23.53m (77ft 2in), Wingspan: 29.20m (95ft 10in), Height: 8.32m (27ft 4in)
Powerplant: Two 1900kW (2550hp) Ivchenko AI-24A turboprop engines
Maximum speed: 540km/h (336mph)
Range: 1850km (1150 miles)
Ceiling: 7700m (25,263ft)
Crew: 2
Maximum payload: 4612kg (10170lb)

TRANSPORT

An-24T
Finished in this overall grey scheme, arguably more appropriate for its status as a tactical transport. Despite its awkward loading arrangements, the sturdy An-24 possessed excellent performance and found ready acceptance with a huge number of operators.

mounted above five ventral fuselage windows. Twenty-six military An-30s were built and were used to map the entirety of Afghanistan in 1982. One VVS example was later equipped with a sampling pod and used to monitor the plume from the Chernobyl nuclear disaster. This An-30 became so radioactive as a result that it was withdrawn immediately afterwards.

Antonov An-30 'Clank'
Weight (maximum take-off): 23,000kg (50,706lb)
Dimensions: Length 24.26m (79ft 7in), Wingspan 29.20m (95ft 10in), Height 8.32m (27ft 4in)
Powerplant: Two 2090kW (2803hp) Ivchenko AI-24TVT turboprop engines
Maximum speed: 540 km/h (340mph)
Range: 2630km (1630 miles)
Ceiling: 8300m (27,200ft)
Crew: 7

An-30
CCCP-30005 was delivered to Aeroflot in 1975, remaining on the State fleet until 1992 when it was sold to Air Transport Europe. Today, this aircraft is preserved in Ukraine.

TRANSPORT

Antonov An-26 'Curl' and An-32 'Cline'

The addition of a rear loading door and ramp transformed the practicality of the basic An-24 design, and the An-26 has proved to be a highly successful tactical transport.

An-26
Intended as a replacement for similarly sized piston powered transports, the An-26 proved an enormous success. Relatively simple, impressively reliable and possessed of excellent performance, the An-26 remains a profoundly useful transport.

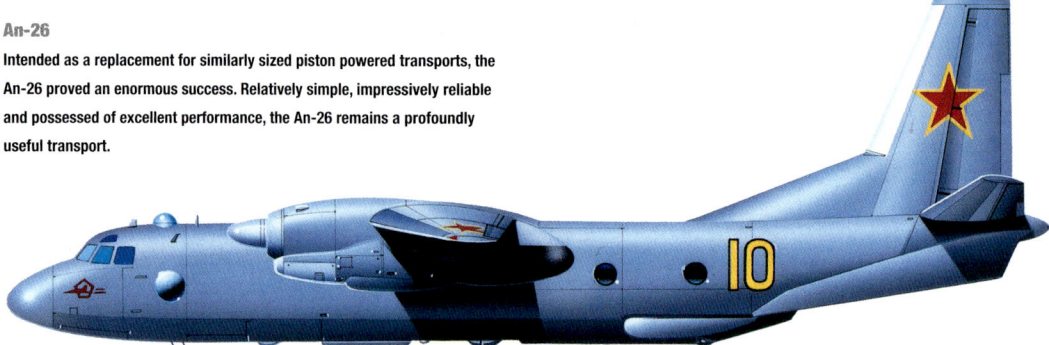

The ventral loading hatch of the An-24T significantly restricted its usefulness, cargo loading and handling proved difficult (particularly in austere or remote locations, and the size of loads was dictated by the ventral hatch dimensions. Antonov OKB were working on the development of an An-24T with a rear cargo ramp before even receiving an official request to develop such a feature. The ramp was ingeniously designed to hinge down to the ground, allowing vehicles to simply drive in or slide under the floor of the cargo bay to allow swift loading of cargo from a truck, simplifying airdrops. When closed, the ramp formed an airtight seal, allowing the cargo hold to be pressurized.

The new rear fuselage was 26cm (10.5in) longer than the An-24, and the ventral fins of the original aircraft had to be replaced with strakes on either side of the base of the cargo ramp. The weight of the airframe increased, so strengthened wings were fitted as well as uprated AI-24VT engines. The first flight of the An-26 was made on 21 May 1969, and serial production began in 1970. Approximately 1400 An-26s had been built when Soviet production ended in 1986, and around half of the aircraft produced went into military service.

An-26
Like the An-24, the An-26 was pressed into a wide variety of specialized roles as well as its basic transport function, including the An-26*Shtabnoy* mobile command post, An-26RTR ELINT aircraft, An-26RT battlefield communications relay aircraft, An-26S VIP transport and An-26Sh navigator trainer. In addition, some aircraft were fitted with extra equipment for arctic operations, and various one-off An-26s have been used for a wide variety of test and trials work. As a reliable transport of useful size, the An-26 was very widely exported, and hundreds remain in use worldwide.

An-32
A development of the An-26, the An-32 is unusual amongst Soviet aircraft in

---

Antonov An-26 'Curl'
Weight (maximum take-off): 24,000kg (52,911lb)
Dimensions: Length 23.8m (78ft 1in), Wingspan 29.3m (96ft 2in), Height 8.58m (28ft 2in)
Powerplant: Two 2,103kW (2,820hp) Progress AI-24VT Turboprop engines and one Tumansky turbojet booster rated at 7.85kN (1760lbf)
Maximum speed: 540km/h (340mph)
Range: 2500km (1600 miles)
Ceiling: 7500m (24,600ft)
Crew: 6
Maximum payload: 5500kg (12,125lb)

TRANSPORT

An-26T
The An-26 was exported to nearly all of the Warsaw Pact nations, including East Germany, and this An-26T served with the East German state carrier Interflug and later with the Luftwaffe after the unification of Germany. It was sold to the Namibian Air Force in 2002.

that it did not originate from a Soviet requirement but instead derived from an Indian request. In the mid-1970s, the Indian military issued a requirement for a medium cargo aircraft that would easily have been answered by the An-26 except for the need for excellent 'hot and high' performance to allow the aircraft to operate in India's mountainous north.

Antonov OKB therefore re-engined the An-26 with two Ivchenko AI-20Ds, an engine that delivered 85 per cent more power than the AI-24VT fitted to the An-26. First flown in July 1976, the An-32 could be instantly distinguished from its predecessor by its much larger nacelles, which placed the engine above rather than forward of the wing. This was necessary to allow clearance for the considerably larger propellers required by the new engine.

Record-maker
The extra power of the An-32 delivered sparkling performance, and in 1985, the aircraft set over 12 world records in its class. Between 1976 and 2012, 373 were built, with India becoming the first customer. Indian crews were highly appreciative of the An-32's excellent performance, and the Indian fleet was upgraded by Antonov in 2009.

Virtually all An-32s were built for export, but the USSR did order a batch of 50 aircraft in 1991, although these were not delivered before the collapse of the Soviet Union, and in the event, they were not taken into Russian service.

An-32B
Shown as it appeared in 1992, this AN-32 was on the strength of Aeroflot. It was later painted in an overall white scheme for humanitarian operations by the United Nations in the Middle East.

An-32B
Weight (maximum take-off): 27,000kg (59,525lb)
Dimensions: Length 23.68m (77ft 8in), Wingspan 29.2m (95ft 10in), Height 8.75m (28ft 8in)
Powerplant: Two 3812kW (5112hp) ZMKB Progress AI-20DM turboprop engines
Maximum speed: 530km/h (330mph)
Range: 2500km (1600 miles)
Ceiling: 9500m (31,200ft)
Crew: 4
Maximum payload: 6700kg (14,770lb)

TRANSPORT

Antonov An-22 'Cock'

The largest turboprop-powered aircraft ever built, the An-22 was designed as a strategic transport and caused a sensation when it appeared at the Paris Air Show in 1965. A handful of An-22s still remain operational in Russia.

An-22

One of seven An-22s built during 1970, CCCP-09325 visited the Paris air show during the early 1970s and survived until 1999. A handful of An-22s remain operational.

The An-22 was developed as a larger aircraft to complement the An-8 and An-12s that were entering service in the late 1950s. A twin-tail configuration was adopted to improve handling in the event of an engine failure and to keep height to a practicable level, and the cargo hold was specifically tailored around the BMD-1 armoured fighting vehicle, the An-22 being able to carry four such vehicles as opposed to the An-12, which can only carry one. At the time of its first flight on 27 February 1965, the An-22 was the largest landplane ever built, and 68 examples of this colossal aircraft had been constructed once production ended in 1976. Surprisingly perhaps, given its unprecedented size, the An-22 possessed the capability to operate from extemporized unpaved airstrips.

Military conversion

Aircraft deliveries were split fairly evenly between Aeroflot and the Soviet Military Airlift Service, the VTA, although the Aeroflot machines are widely believed to have been primarily used for military duties as well. Conversion of the first military unit to operate the An-22 took place in 1974, by which time the aircraft had already been used to deliver Soviet humanitarian aid to Peru in the aftermath of the Ancash earthquake in 1970. An-22s were also used to fly military supplies to Egypt and Syria during the Yom Kippur War of 1973, as well as to Angola in 1975 and Ethiopia in 1977. The Soviet invasion of Afghanistan in 1979 saw An-22s utilized to deliver airborne troops, and the aircraft flew regular supply flights for the duration of the conflict, with one being lost near Kabul in October 1984.

Still serving

The An-22 comfortably outlived the USSR, and Russia intends to fly the aircraft until at least 2033. Proposed developments of the An-22 included an amphibian equipped with hydroplanes and a 724-seat double deck transport, but neither of these made it past the design stage.

An-22 'Cock'

Weight (maximum take-off): 250,000kg (551,156lb)
Dimensions: Length 57.92m (190ft), Wingspan 64.4m (211ft 3in), Height 12.53m (41ft 1in)
Powerplant: Four 11,000kW (15,000hp) Kuznetsov NK-12MA turboprop engines
Maximum speed: 740km/h (460mph)
Range: 5000km (3100 miles)
Ceiling: 9100m (29,900ft)
Crew: 5–6
Maximum payload: 80,000kg (176,370lb)

Ilyushin Il-76 'Candid', Il-78 'Midas' and A-50 'Mainstay'

The archetypical Soviet transport of the 1970s and '80s, the rugged Il-76 has enjoyed great success as a strategic transport as well as proving amenable to modification for a wide range of roles.

The Il-76 answered a 1966 request for an airborne assault transport able to deliver 33,000kg (72,752lb) load over 5000km (3106 miles) and to be able to operate from unprepared runways. Making its first flight on 25 March 1971, the initial production Il-76 appeared in May 1973. After around 80 aircraft had been built, production switched to the Il-76M, which featured a reinforced structure, more fuel, a widened rear fuselage and an increased maximum payload.

In 1981, production then changed to a variant with a further strengthened airframe and greater payload capacity: the Il-76MD. The Il-76 formed the backbone of the Soviet Union's transport fleet throughout the last two decades of its existence, and exports were made to a swathe of nations, but only India and Libya obtained significant quantities, receiving 24 examples each. In Indian service, the Il-76MDs were given the impressive name of *Gajraj*, which roughly translates as 'King Elephant'. On operations, the Il-76 delivered excellent service in frequently difficult conditions, although in Afghanistan, the aircraft proved vulnerable to mujahideen MANPADS, particularly the US-supplied Stinger.

Long service

Existing Il-76s have been subject to further post-Soviet upgrades, and the aircraft remains in production in 2024, with later examples powered by significantly more economical PS-90 high-bypass turbofan engines.

Just under 1000 examples had been constructed at the time of writing. The aircraft remains an important part of the Russian Aerospace Forces and continues to be used operationally, including with both Ukraine and Russia during the Russian invasion. In addition to its standard transport function, the Il-76 was also used during the Soviet era as a SAR aircraft, a firefighting aircraft,

Il-76MD

The most important Soviet strategic transport aircraft from the 1970s onwards, the Il-76 has seen a huge amount of operational service over the last 50 years. Following the break-up of the Soviet Union, this aircraft, CCCP-76732, entered service with the Ukrainian Air Force.

Ilyushin Il-76 'Candid'
Weight (maximum take-off): 190,000kg (418,878lb)
Dimensions: Length 46.59m (152ft 10in), Wingspan 50.5m (165ft 8in), Height 14.76m (48ft 5in)
Powerplant: Four Soloviev D-30KP turbofan engines, each rated at 117.7kN (26,500lbf)
Maximum speed: 850km/h (528mph)
Range: 4200km (2610 miles) with max payload
Ceiling: 12,000m (39,370ft)
Crew: 6–7
Armament: Two 23mm (0.91in) Gryazev-Shipunov GSh-23L cannon flexibly mounted in tail turret
Maximum payload: 48,000kg (105,822lb)

TRANSPORT

an airborne laser weapon testbed (designated the Beriev A-60), a missile tracking platform, an ELINT aircraft, a Zero-G cosmonaut trainer and as a mobile hospital.

Ilyushin Il-78 and Beriev A-50

Work on a tanker version of the Il-76 began before the prototype even flew, but its actual existence was delayed until the appearance of the Il-76MD. With a refuelling operator replacing the rear gunner in the tail position, the Il-78, as it was designated, made its first flight on 26 June 1983, entering service in June 1987. Today, the Il-78 fleet is used primarily to refuel Russian Tu-95 and Tu-160 aircraft. An AEW&C variant was also developed, the modification work for this variant being carried out by Beriev; thus the aircraft is designated the Beriev A-50.

Combining the airframe of the Il-76MD with a rotodome-mounted E-821 *Shmel* (bumblebee) radar, the A-50 is able to search for a fighter-sized target up to a range of 230km (143 miles) at low altitude. Twenty-four A-50s are believed to have been built, of which around nine are conjectured to remain in service. Another very specialized variant, of which only two examples were built, is the Il-82 strategic radio relay aircraft that operates in concert with the Il-80 (featuring a similar large canoe-shaped fairing atop the forward fuselage) as part of wartime nuclear command and control and which can communicate with satellites and submerged submarines.

Ilyushin Il-76 'Candid'
Weight (maximum take-off): 190,000kg (418,878lb)
Dimensions: Length 46.59m (152ft 10in), Wingspan 50.5m (165ft 8in), Height 14.76m (48ft 5in)
Powerplant: Four Soloviev D-30KP turbofan engines, each rated at 117.7kN (26,500lbf)
Maximum speed: 850km/h (528mph)
Range: 4200km (2610 miles) with max payload
Ceiling: 12,000m (39,370ft)
Crew: 6–7
Armament: Two 23mm (0.91in) Gryazev-Shipunov GSh-23L cannon flexibly mounted in tail turret
Maximum payload: 48,000kg (105,822lb)

Il-76TD
The impressive rough-field capability of the Il-76 is enhanced by its 20-wheel undercarriage, particularly evident when viewed head-on. The extensive nose glazing is unusual to Western eyes but delivers outstanding visibility to the navigator's position.

TRANSPORT

Il-76MD

'01 Red' was the support aircraft for the 'Russian Knights' display team in the early 1990s and was therefore much photographed in the West, even before the dissolution of the Soviet Union. This aircraft visited RAF Leuchars in Scotland in September 1991.

A-50

Entering service in the mid-1980s, the A-50 replaced the Tu-126 'Moss' in the airborne early warning and control role. Its existence was revealed to the West by the Soviet electronics engineer and spy Adolf Tolkachev.

Beriev A-50 'Mainstay'

Weight (Maximum take-off): 170,000kg (374,786lb)
Dimensions: Length 49.59m (162ft 8in), Wingspan 50.5m (165ft 8in), Height 14.76m (48ft 5in)
Powerplant: Four Soloviev D-30KP turbofan engines, each rated at 117.7kN (26,500lbf)
Maximum speed: 900km/h (560mph)
Range: 7500km (4700 miles)
Ceiling: 12,000m (39,000ft)
Crew: 15

A-50

The A-50 outlived the nation that created it by several decades and in early 2024 the Russian Air Force is believed to retain six operational A-50s on strength. '50 Red' is one of the aircraft updated in the 2000s to A-50U standard with new electronics and avionics.

TRANSPORT

Antonov An-124 'Condor'

Another enormous transport fielded by the Soviet Union, the An-124 had only been in service for around five years when the USSR ceased to exist. The aircraft remains the largest military transport in service.

In 1968, the Lockheed C-5 Galaxy succeeded the An-22 as the world's largest aircraft, but the American aircraft would not remain so for long. Design work for what became the An-124 began in 1971, and the aircraft made its first flight on 24 December 1982. The aircraft was slightly shorter than the C-5, but with a greater wingspan, and could carry a significantly heavier payload.

The two aircraft resemble each other quite closely, but the An-124 features a conventional, low set horizontal tailplane and a remarkable 20 main wheels, allowing for rough field operations. The nose gear consists of two sets of twin wheel units, which steer independently and can 'kneel' to facilitate loading and unloading. As well as the huge cargo bay, the An-124 features a pressurized passenger section with 88 seats behind the wing.

From the start, the An-124 was fitted with a quadruplex fly-by-wire system. Entering service in 1986, the An-124's Lotarev D-18T engines initially proved unreliable, although this has greatly improved over time, and a total of 54 An-124s were built by the time production ceased in 2004.

Shortly after its existence was disclosed, the An-124 set 21 world records. Understandably, however, Soviet military use of the An-124 was limited: the aircraft was officially commissioned into service in March 1991, and the Soviet Union collapsed only nine months later. The An-124, and its spectacular six-engined development, the unique An-225, subsequently saw much use as commercial heavy lift aircraft. Russian Aerospace Forces, the sole military user, reportedly maintained a fleet of 12 An-124s in 2019, with a further 14 in reserve.

An-124 'Condor'

Weight (maximum take-off): 402,000kg (886,258lb)
Dimensions: Length 69.1m (226ft 8in), Wingspan 73.3m (240ft 6in), Height 21.08m (69ft 2in)
Powerplant: Four Progress D-18T turbofan engines, each rated at 229kN (51000lbf)
Maximum speed: 865km/h (537mph)
Range: 14,000km (8700 miles)
Ceiling: 12,000m (39,000ft)
Crew: 6–7
Maximum payload: 150,000kg (330,693lb)

An-124

'10 Black' was one of two An-124s that visited the Farnborough airshow in the UK, in 1990, just before the end of the Soviet Era. The An-124 is one of relatively few Soviet designs to enjoy a successful commercial career after 1992.

Antonov An-72 and An-74 'Coaler'

The distinctive An-72 was intended as a STOL transport with good rough field capability. The related An-74 was specifically intended for Arctic operations.

Initially flown on 22 December 1977, the An-72 featured two Ivchenko D-36 high bypass turbofans mounted in such a way that the jet exhaust flows over the wing, increasing lift due to the Coandă effect and allowing the An-72 to take off in around 620m (2000ft) and land in just 420m (1400ft). From the front, the engines gave the impression of enormous circular ears, leading to the aircraft being nicknamed "*Cheburashka*" due to its resemblance to the iconic Soviet cartoon character. Evaluation of the aircraft proved protracted, and the An-72 only entered service in 1988, proving popular with aircrew due to its superlative STOL performance and good handling but less so with service personnel due to the awkward engine placement.

AN-74

Developed in tandem with the An-72, the An-74 was a civil development intended for operations in the Arctic and Antarctic. It can be fitted with wheel-ski landing gear, upgraded de-icing equipment and other equipment to allow it to deliver cargo and passengers to unprepared airstrips

An-72

The unusual engine placement of the An-72 was chosen primarily to increase lift but this layout also lessened the chances of foreign object ingestion, important when operating from unprepared airstrips.

in conditions ranging from -60 to 45 degrees Celsius (-76 to 113 degrees Fahrenheit) and operate at very high and low latitudes, including over both poles. Despite its civil origins, a military transport derivative was developed and remains in service with Russia, along with the An-72. Production of both types was modest, though small numbers continued to be produced after the dissolution of the USSR. To date, a combined total of 195 aircraft has been built, and more may yet be ordered.

AWACS variant

An AWACS variant with a rotodome mounted above a strikingly swept forward vertical tail, designated the An-71, was also built, and was intended for carrier operations; it never entered production but still received the NATO reporting name Madcap.

Antonov An-72
Weight (maximum take-off): 34,500kg (76,060lb)
Dimensions: Length 28.07m (92ft 1in), Wingspan 31.89m (104ft 8in), Height 8.65m (28ft 5in)
Powerplant: Two Lotarev D-36 turbofan engines, each rated at 63.9kN (14330lbf)
Maximum speed: 700 km/h (435mph)
Range: 4325km (2688/miles)
Ceiling: 10,000m (32,808ft)
Crew: 5
Maximum payload: 10,000kg (22,000lb)

HELICOPTERS

After a slow start, the USSR came to dominate the world of rotorcraft, developing the world's most produced helicopter in the form of the Mi-8 and the world's largest helicopter to enter serial production, the Mi-26. Although the products of Mil OKB represent 95 per cent of the USSR's rotorcraft output, Kamov managed to carve out a niche by producing helicopters for the Navy. The following helicopters feature in this chapter:

- Mil Mi-1 'Hare'
- Mil Mi-4 'Hound'
- Yakovlev Yak-24 'Horse'
- Mil Mi-6 'Hook' and Mi-10 'Harke'
- Kamov Ka-25 'Hormone'
- Kamov K-27 and Ka-29 'Helix'
- Mil Mi-2 'Hoplite'
- Mil Mi-8 'Hip'
- Mil Mi-14 'Haze'
- Mil Mi-24 'Hind'
- Mil Mi-26 'Halo'

An image designed to give NATO planners nightmares throughout the 1970s and 1980s as Soviet troops advance from the ubiquitous Mi-8 during an exercise in typical northern European countryside. After initially lagging behind Western rotorcraft, the Soviet Union enthusiastically adopted the helicopter for a swathe of battlefield roles.

HELICOPTERS

Mil Mi-1 'Hare'

The Soviet Union's first production helicopter, the Mi-1, proved an incredible success for such a pioneering design, with around 1800 built in the USSR as well as over 1500 licence-built in Poland.

Mikhail Mil had been active in rotary-wing development since the 1930s, but detailed design work on his first truly successful helicopter, originally designated the GM-1, was begun in 1946. The first untethered flight occurred on 20 September 1948, and following a competition between the GM-1, Yak-100 and Bratukhin B-11 in which the GM-1 was judged the winner, 15 production machines were ordered in 1950. The Mi-1 was revealed in public at the Tushino air display of 1951, following which it received the reporting name 'Hare'. Initial production Mi-1s were followed by the Mi-1 *Moskvich*, which was a standard Mi-1 with added soundproofing and a metal rotor as well as other upgrades for use by Aeroflot. Eventually, this version became the production standard, and was referred to simply as the Mi-1.

Later production Mi-1s were of the Mi-1T variant with uprated AI-26V engine and other minor improvements. The dual control Mil-1U and Mi-1P float-equipped amphibian also saw production. However, the Mi-1MU, an armed variant fitted with four 3M11

Mil Mi-1U 'Hare'
Weight (maximum take-off): 2330kg (5137lb)
Dimensions: Length 12.09m (39ft 8in), Rotor diameter 14.35m (47ft 1in), Height 3.3m (10ft 10in)
Powerplant: One 429kW (575hp) Ivchenko AI-26V seven-cylinder air-cooled radial piston engine
Maximum speed: 185km/h (115mph)
Range: 430km (267 miles)
Ceiling: 3500m (11,483ft)
Crew: 1 or 2

Falanga or six 9M14 *Malyutka* anti-tank missiles, did not progress beyond the prototype stage. The Mi-1 was used by several branches of the Soviet armed forces for many years in a wide range of roles including observation, liaison, search and rescue (SAR), air ambulance and flight training. This useful little helicopter eventually served with the armed forces of over 20 nations.

From 1956, licence production took place by WSK PZL-Swidnik in Poland under the designation SM-1, and a five-seat variant with new fuselage was produced as the SM-2 in Poland, though less than 100 were built.

Mi-1U
Pictured as it appeared in 1973, this dual control Mi-1U was operated by the Volunteer Society for Cooperation with the Army, Aviation and Navy (DOSAAF), a paramilitary cadet organisation that was disbanded in 1991.

Mil Mi-4 'Hound'

Superficially resembling the Sikorsky H-19, the Mi-4 was a larger and more powerful helicopter and was built in greater numbers. The Mi-4 formed the backbone of Soviet Army Aviation until its replacement by the Mi-8.

Initially flying in April 1952, the Mi-4 entered service in the following year and was originally fitted with wooden skinned rotor blades that could only be used for the underwhelming total of 100 hours. This had been raised to 600 hours by 1957, but the introduction of all-metal blades in 1960 permitted a life of 1500 hours. The Mi-4 was also fitted with hydraulically boosted flight controls, a first for a Soviet helicopter, and in military service the Mi-4 proved highly successful, demonstrating excellent load-carrying ability, great strength and a high standard of reliability. By the time production ended in the Soviet Union in 1968, around 3500 Mi-4s had been built, most for military use, and over the course of its production life, the Mi-4 had been used as the basis for a host of variants.

Assault versions

As well as the basic Mi-4 utility transport, which received the reporting name Hound-A, Mil produced the Mi-4A assault transport and the armed Mi-4AV, which could carry four 9M17M ATGM *Falanga* anti-tank missiles and 96 57mm (2.24in) NAR S-5M unguided rockets, or six 100kg (220lb) bombs or four 250kg (551lb) bombs. Hound-B and Hound-C were both ASW variants, the Mi-4M and Mi-4PL respectively, which featured search radar and sonar equipment, but most Mi-4 variants never received a specific reporting name from NATO, being referred to simply as Hounds or Hound-As.

Variants

Other major variants included: the Mi-4L, a six-seat VIP transport that could also be converted into an air ambulance or fire-fighting helicopter; the Mi-4PS search-and-rescue helicopter; the Mi-4T, which was a military transport version built in large numbers that featured a larger diameter rotor and bulged windows; the Mi-4BT float-equipped minesweeper; the Mi-4KK and KU, which were both mobile command posts; the Mi-4MK ECM aircraft; and the Mi-4U target designator helicopter. There was even a radio-controlled target drone variant, the Mi-4UM. Manifold trials machines and specialized variants were built in

Mi-4A

Armed with a single 12.7mm (0.5in) A-12.7 machine gun in the ventral gondola, the Mi-4A was the first dedicated assault transport variant to be developed from the basic Mi-4 design. Later Mi-4s would feature more powerful armament, including rockets and missiles.

Mil Mi-4A 'Hound'

Weight (maximum take-off): 7550kg (16,645lb)
Dimensions: Length 16.8m (55ft 1in), Rotor diameter 21m (68ft 11in), Height 4.4m (14ft 5in)
Powerplant: One 1250kW (1680hp) Shvetsov ASh-82V 14-cylinder air-cooled radial piston engine
Maximum speed: 185km/h (115mph)
Range: 500km (310 miles)
Ceiling: 5500m (18,000ft)
Crew: 1 or 2
Maximum payload: up to 1600kg (3527lb)
Armament: One optional 12.7mm (0.5in) TKB-481M machine gun flexibly mounted in ventral gondola

HELICOPTERS

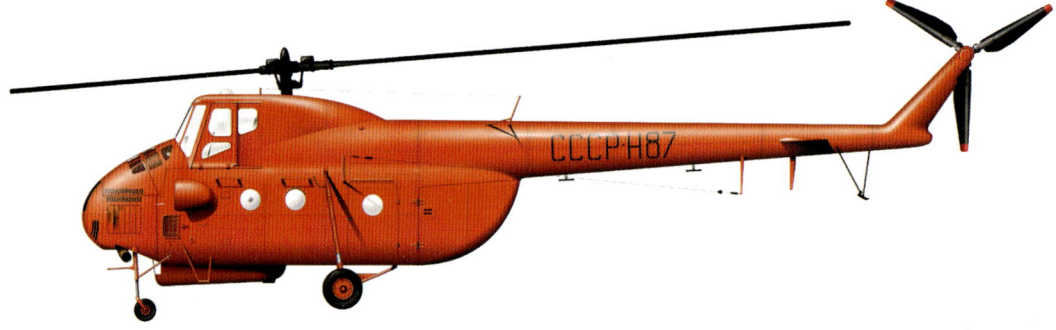

very small numbers along with a large number of civil versions. Substantial quantities of demilitarized Mi-4s were also taken into various civil roles as they were withdrawn from the armed forces.

Widely exported

As with most sufficiently effective Soviet equipment, the Mi-4 was very widely exported. All of the Warsaw Pact nations operated the type, and a large number of aligned nations also took delivery of the Mi-4. One such user was China, which also started local production as the Harbin Z-5 after being supplied with drawings in 1958, building 558 aircraft.

Chinese engineers developed a turbine-powered variant with a single Dongan WZ-5 turboshaft engine-mounted just under the cabin and with the cockpit relocated to the nose. Appearing in 1969, only 11 were ever built. The Chinese also flew at least one Mi-4 with a Pratt & Whitney Canada PT6T-6 turboshaft engine in 1979, but production did not proceed.

Most users replaced the Mi-4 over the course of the 1960s and '70s with the turbine powered Mi-8, but the Hound lingered on in several air arms. The last operational examples were thought to have been withdrawn by

Mi-4

CCCP-H87 took part in the first Soviet Antarctic Expedition in 1957. It would not survive long however, being written off at Mirny Station, Queen Mary Land, Antarctica in January of the following year.

Albania in 2005, though some North Korean examples were filmed being flown in 2014 and may remain in limited service.

Soviet naval personnel descend a rope ladder from a Mil Mi-4 'Hound' onto the deck of a surfaced 'Whiskey' class submarine.

Mil Mi-4 'Hound'

Weight (maximum take-off): 7550kg (16,645lb)
Dimensions: Length 16.8m (55ft 1in), Rotor diameter 21m (68ft 11in), Height 4.4m (14ft 5in)
Powerplant: One 1250kW (1680hp) Shvetsov ASh-82V 14-cylinder air-cooled radial piston engine
Maximum speed: 185km/h (115mph)
Range: 500km (310 miles)
Ceiling: 5500m (18,000ft)
Crew: 1 or 2
Maximum payload: up to 1600kg (3527lb)

Yakovlev Yak-24 'Horse'

An early rival to the dominance of Mil in helicopter development was Yakovlev, but ultimately, the Yak-24 would become Yakovlev's only rotary winged aircraft to enter production and service.

In 1947, Yakovlev flew their first experimental helicopter, the EG-1, featuring a co-axial rotor, and later, the Yak-100, which bore an uncanny resemblance to the Sikorsky S-51, was unsuccessfully submitted as a competitor to the Mi-1. Yakovlev completely changed tack for the Yak-24, which was a twin-engine, twin-rotor heavy-lift helicopter.

Record-breaking size

When it performed its first free flight on 3 July 1952, it was the largest helicopter in the world and capable of carrying 30 troops or 18 stretchers and medical attendants or up to 2 tonnes (4409lb) of cargo. The boxy fuselage featured a rear door with a ramp for driving in light vehicles. For defence, a TKB-481 12.7mm (0.5in) machine gun could be installed on a flexible mounting in the nose. Yak-24 prototypes set several load-to-altitude records in the early 1950s, and the helicopter was approved for production in 1956.

Initial production aircraft were followed by the improved Yak-24U, which featured a strengthened fuselage of greater width and wider rotor blades, allowing it to lift a payload of up to four

Yak-24

An early production Yak 24, '35 Yellow' features a canvas skin and early tail unit, later production aircraft were fitted with endplate fins. This helicopter also lacks the nose mounted 12.7mm (0.5in) machine gun.

Yakovlev Yak-24 'Horse'
Weight (maximum take-off): 15,830kg (34,899lb)
Dimensions: Length 22.4m (73ft 6in), Rotor diameter 20m (65ft 7in), Height 6.5m (21ft 4in)
Powerplant: Two 1300kW (1700hp) Shvetsov ASh-82V 14-cylinder air-cooled radial piston engines
Maximum speed: 175km/h (109mph)
Range: 380km (240 miles)
Ceiling: 4000m (13,000ft)
Crew: 3
Maximum payload: 4000kg (8800lb)

tonnes (8800lb). The Yak-24U could be distinguished externally by its flat tailplane, eliminating the dihedral of the Yak-24. In addition, the Yak-24K VIP transport, a single example of the Yak-24A civil airliner variant and an intriguing tactical pipeline-laying variant, the Yak-24T, were all produced. In service, the Yak-24 proved somewhat disappointing, and its operational life was short. Total production numbers are unknown, but no more than 100 examples were built in total.

HELICOPTERS

Mil Mi-6 'Hook' and Mi-10 'Harke'

For many years the largest and fastest production helicopter in the world, the Mil Mi-6 was also the first Soviet helicopter to be powered by turboshaft engines. Both the Mi-6 and its flying crane derivative, the Mi-10, remained in service until the early 2000s.

The Mi-6 derived from a joint civil and military requirement for a very large transport helicopter capable of carrying an 11 tonne (25,000lb) payload over a distance of 240km (150 miles). Flying for the first time on 5 June 1957, the helicopter was ordered into production in 1960 despite the fact that flight trials were not completed until 1962. Eventually 924 examples of the big helicopter were produced during a lengthy production run, with the last rolled out in 1980.

Initially flown with prominent wheel spats, production Mi-6s dispensed with this feature but added the distinctive stub wings to the first pre-production aircraft. The wings, which were detachable, spanned some 15.3m (50ft 2in) and provided around 20 per cent of necessary lift during cruising flight as well as making the helicopter instantly recognizable.

Record breaker

Early in its career, the Mi-6 broke many speed and payload records. For example, in 1961, it won the Sikorsky Trophy for the first helicopter to exceed 300km/h (186mph), and the record it set in 1962 for carrying a five-tonne (11,023lb) payload over a 1000km (621.4km) distance at 284km/h (176mph) still stands in 2024. In service, the Mi-6 proved somewhat underpowered, and the aircraft usually required a take-off roll when loaded. It was also prone to excessive vibration at low speed but nonetheless proved generally effective as a heavy lift helicopter and in a variety of specialist roles.

Mil Mi-10PP
Weight (maximum take-off): 39,800kg (87,744lb)
Dimensions: Length 32.86m (107ft 10in), Rotor diameter 35m (114ft 10in)
Powerplant: Two 4100kW (5500shp) Soloviev D-25V turboshaft engines
Maximum speed: 300km/h (190mph)
Range: 600km (373 miles)
Ceiling: 4500m (14,800ft)
Crew: 6

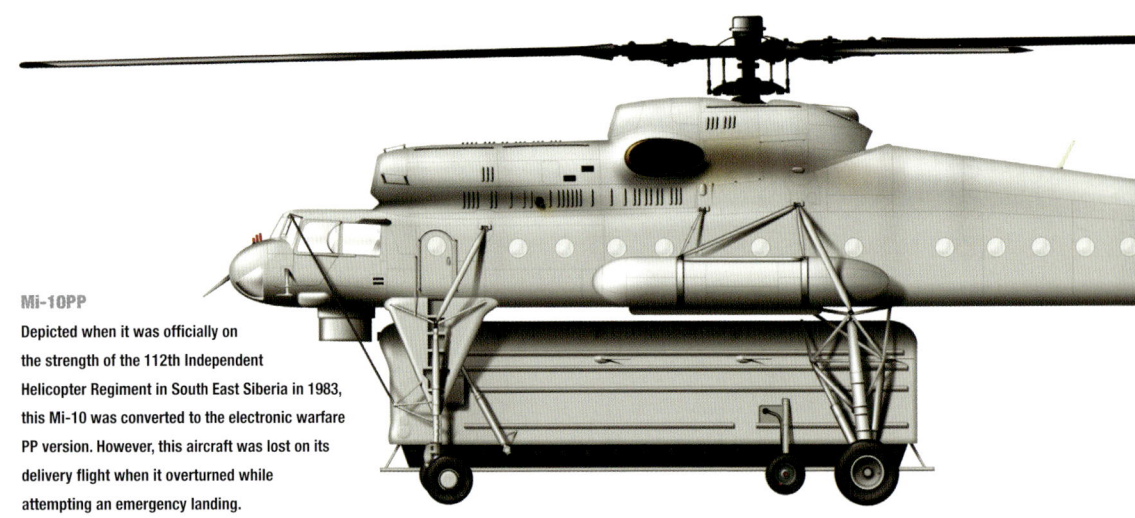

Mi-10PP
Depicted when it was officially on the strength of the 112th Independent Helicopter Regiment in South East Siberia in 1983, this Mi-10 was converted to the electronic warfare PP version. However, this aircraft was lost on its delivery flight when it overturned while attempting an emergency landing.

HELICOPTERS

Mil Mi-6 'Hook'
Weight (maximum take-off): 44,000kg (97,003lb)
Dimensions: Length 33.18m (108ft 10in), Rotor diameter 35m (114ft 10in), Height 9.16m (30ft)
Powerplant: Two 4100kW (5500shp) Soloviev D-25V turboshaft engines
Maximum speed: 300km/h (190mph)
Range: 970km (600 miles)
Ceiling: 4500m (14,800ft)
Crew: 6
Maximum payload: 12,000kg (26,455lb)

As well as the standard Mi-6, Mi-6A, and Mi-6T cargo helicopters, the Mi-6 also served in the SAR (search and rescue) role as the Mi-6APS and the Mi-6PS, which was specifically tailored to recover Vostok and Soyuz space modules. Other variants included an airborne firefighting version, the Mi-6PZh2, and the Mi-6TZ fuel transport helicopter amongst others. The Mi-6 was quite widely exported, flying with just over a dozen other nations. Vietnam was an early user and utilized its Mi-6s to transport jet fighter aircraft slung under the fuselage to hidden remote locations rather than leaving them on airfields where they would be vulnerable to US strikes. The Mi-6s would then fly them back again when required.

Mi-6
Built in 1971, this Mi-6 displays considerable weathering, typical of Mi-6s in service. The Mi-6 remained the world's largest production helicopter until the appearance of the Mi-26.

Mi-10 flying crane
Mil also developed the Mi-10 flying crane from the Mi-6, which first flew on 15 June 1960. The initial model featured a strikingly tall undercarriage intended to carry load pallets or other bulky cargo between its legs, a feature demonstrated at the Paris Air Show, where the Mi-10 flew with a LAZ bus carried between the undercarriage legs. Later Mi-10s featured a much shorter and lighter undercarriage and a second rearward-facing cockpit with full flight controls mounted ventrally under the nose from which a pilot could accurately position underslung loads.

Its specialized nature meant that only 55 Mi-10s were built in total, enjoying some success in VVS units, in which they were mainly used to carry bulky ECM equipment. A single civil example was exported to Bolivia to become the sole Mi-10 sold to an overseas customer.

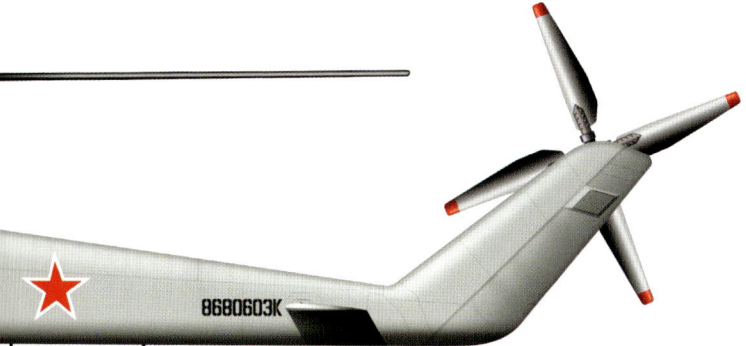

HELICOPTERS

Kamov Ka-25 'Hormone'

From the late 1960s onwards, the Ka-25 became the Soviet Union's standard shipboard helicopter, serving on Soviet vessels from April 1967 until the end of the Cold War and beyond.

Ka-25Ts
'70 Red' served with Soviet Naval Aviation during the mid 1970s. This is an early production example of the Ka-25Ts variant, developed to provide over-the-horizon, targeting information for ship- and submarine-launched surface-to-surface missiles.

The co-axial rotor system championed by Kamov and utilized by the Ka-25 obviates the need for a tail rotor and makes for a compact airframe, ideal for shipboard use where space is at a premium. Whilst Mil designs dominated the Red Army, Kamov became the de facto supplier of rotorcraft to the Soviet Navy. The tiny single-seat Ka-10 'Hat' became the first Soviet helicopter to operate from a ship, and a small number of the two-seat Ka-15 'Hen' were operated by the service in the utility role, but this aircraft was too small to carry any sort of offensive armament. The Ka-25 was of a different calibre entirely and answered an urgent need to provide Soviet warships with a capable ASW and multipurpose helicopter.

Initially flown on 20 May 1961, the Ka-25 entered service in its initial Ka-25PL form in the ASW role, carrying a search radar in a prominent chin-mounted radome, an Oka-2 dipping sonar and a MAD pod under the tail. The offensive weaponry of the Ka-25 consisted of two homing torpedoes, or depth charges, carried in a detachable ventral weapons bay, and a wire reel could be mounted on the forward fuselage for controlling wire-guided torpedoes if these were carried. This initial variant was allocated the reporting name Hormone-A by NATO and saw most of its service operating from Kiev-class guided-missile cruisers.

Variants

Two other major variants were also produced, the Ka-25T (Hormone-B) and the Ka-25PS (Hormone-C). The former variant was used for missile targeting. The Soviet Navy aimed to neutralize Western Naval superiority by means of cruise missiles, but these had to be guided onto their target. The Ka-25T featured a larger radome, housing a more powerful radar that would be used to illuminate a target for missiles. The undercarriage of this variant was retractable to remove it from the radar's sweep, and a datalink for communicating with missiles was housed under a small radome at the rear of the fuselage. All other combat equipment and armament was deleted, as it was in the Ka-25PS, apart from the search radar. This was a search-and-rescue variant, though it could also be used as a utility transport, equipped with tip up seats for up to 12 passengers, extra external fuel tanks, a rescue winch, searchlight and loudspeaker. Moreover, the Ka-25PS fleet was generally painted in a red and

Kamov Ka-25Ts
Weight (maximum take-off): 7150kg (15,763lb)
Dimensions: Length 9.75m (32ft), Rotor diameter 15.74m (51ft 8in), Height 5.37m (17ft 7in)
Powerplant: Two 671kW (900shp) Glushenkov GTD-3F turboshaft engines
Maximum speed: 205km/h (127mph)
Range: 700km (435 miles)
Ceiling: 3500m (11,483ft)
Crew: 2

114

white high-visibility colour scheme. In addition to these versions of the Ka-25, a Ka-25BShZ minesweeping variant was built in very small numbers, and a solitary civil Ka-25K flying crane version was demonstrated at the Paris air show in 1967, but no production followed. A proposed Red Army assault version with a glazed nose, skid undercarriage, cargo compartment, under fuselage turret and provision for rocket and missile armament was proposed as the Ka-25F but lost out to the Mi-24 'Hind'.

In total, 460 Ka-25s had been built when production ended in 1975, and as well as flying for the Soviet Navy, these served in the post-Soviet states of Russia and Ukraine after 1991 as well as being exported to Bulgaria, Yugoslavia, Syria, India and Vietnam.

Kamov Ka-27 and Ka-29 'Helix'

Although retaining the same layout as the Ka-25, the Ka-27 was a considerably more powerful and capable helicopter. Unusually amongst Soviet military aircraft, its civil derivative has proved quite successful with Western operators in the years following the end of the Cold War.

The Kamov Ka-25 had proved successful but was always viewed as somewhat underpowered. Work on a successor got underway during 1969, resulting in the Ka-27, which performed its first flight on 24 December 1973. Trials and development work were somewhat drawn out, and the new helicopter eventually entered service with the Soviet Navy in April 1981, receiving the reporting name 'Helix'.

Retaining the same configuration as the Ka-25, with Kamov's trademark co-axial double rotor, the Ka-27 featured engines with over twice the power of the earlier helicopter despite weighing

Ka-27PL

Operating with the 83rd Anti-Submarine Warfare Regiment in 1991, this Ka-27PL displays three silhouettes of NATO submarines claimed as detected during exercises, as well as the Polar Bear and Polar Star markings of the Soviet Northern Fleet.

only around a quarter more. The boxier fuselage offered a greater internal volume, though the external dimensions and footprint of the Ka-27 were much the same as the Ka-25.

Avionics and systems were more modern, more fuel was carried and the airframe incorporated new materials,

Kamov K-27PL

Weight (maximum take-off): 12,000kg (26,455lb)
Dimensions: Length 12.25m (40ft 2in), Rotor diameter 5.8m (51ft 10in), Height 5.4m (17ft 9in)
Powerplant: Two 1659kW (2225shp) Klimov TV3-117KM turboshaft engines
Maximum speed: 291km/h (181mph)
Range: 760km (472 miles)
Ceiling: 5000m (16,000ft)
Crew: 2–3
Armament: Up to 800kg (1764lb) of bombs, torpedoes, mines or other stores
Maximum payload: Up to 4000kg (8800lb) internally or 5000kg (11,000lb) as a slung load

HELICOPTERS

such as titanium and composites. The initial production variant, the Ka-27PL, was – like the initial Ka-25s – an ASW platform. The sensor suite included: an *Osminog* (Octopus) search radar in a bulbous undernose radome; sonobuoys; dipping sonar; and an electronic support measures (ESM) locator. It was capable of carrying four homing torpedoes or guided ASW bombs in the weapons bay.

The Ka-27 also featured a sealed lower hull intended to keep the helicopter afloat if it proved necessary to ditch at sea. The Ka-27PL was offered for export with extra fuel tanks fitted on either side of the fuselage and a slightly less capable systems suite as the Ka-28, although deliveries only began to export customers after the end of the Cold War.

A SAR variant, the Ka-27PS, was produced at the same time with all ASW equipment removed, with the exception of the search radar, but with more fuel and featuring 12 folding seats or four stretchers in its cabin as well as a 300kg (660lb) winch.

Kamov Ka-29

The basic Ka-27 design was used to develop a family of specialist helicopters, beginning with the Ka-29

Ka-29

'71 Red' is depicted in the colours of the 830th Independent Shipborne Anti-Submarine Helicopter Regiment, based in Murmansk, during the difficult years immediately following the collapse of the Soviet Union. The Russian Naval ensign has replaced the Soviet ensign on the fuselage side.

ship-based assault helicopter. Easily distinguishable from the base model Helix by its wider, more angular forward fuselage, and its windscreen that consists of three flat panels rather than the two curved sections of the Ka-27, the Ka-29 contains a cabin with space for 12 to 16 troops (or four stretchers and eight passengers). The maiden flight of the Ka-29 occurred on 28 July 1976, and the aircraft was commissioned into the Soviet Navy in August 1987.

AEW variant

An AEW variant was also produced as the Ka-31, featuring a large radar dish under the fuselage. While it first flew in 1987, this variant only entered service after the dissolution of the Soviet Union.

A civilian variant, the Ka-32, has also been derived from the Ka-27, and this has enjoyed success on the global market due to its exceptional power to weight ratio, rugged construction and reliability. Examples fly with various operators in Canada, South Korea and Switzerland, amongst others.

Kamov Ka-29 'Helix'

Weight (maximum take-off): 11,500kg (25,353lb)
Dimensions: Length 11.6m (38ft), Rotor diameter 15.9m (52ft), Height 5.4m (17ft 8in)
Powerplant: Two 1660kW (2230shp) Klimov TV3-117V turboshaft engines
Maximum speed: 280km/h (174mph)
Range: 800km (497 miles)
Ceiling: 5000m (16,000ft)
Crew: 1–3
Armament: One 7.62mm (0.3in) machine gun or one 30mm (1.18in) A242 cannon flexibly mounted in nose; up to 2000kg (4400lb) bombs, rockets, missiles or stores

Mil Mi-2 'Hoplite'

A turbine-powered derivative of the Mi-1, the Mi-2 proved even more successful and was built in large numbers. Many examples remain in service today.

Flown for the first time on 22 September 1961, the Mi-2 saw the Ivchenko radial engine of the Mi-1 replaced with a pair of Klimov GTD-350 turboshafts, which together weighed about half the mass of the piston engine but developed around 40 per cent more power. As a result, the performance of the helicopter was transformed and payload more than doubled. The turbines were mounted above rather than within the fuselage as on the Mi-1, resulting in much more space in the cabin. Initially, the Mi-2 was fitted with the rotor, rotorhead and tail unit of the Mi-1, but later production machines utilized a new rotor constructed of fibreglass. Apart from the first prototypes that were built by Mil in Moscow, all Mi-2s were built in Poland by PZL-Świdnik, and ultimately, 5497 were built by the time production ended in 1998.

PZL versions

Over 20 variants were subsequently developed by PZL for both civil and military purposes, including a variety of missile-armed and gunship versions for the Polish armed forces. Those supplied to the Soviet Union were of two major types: the basic multipurpose utility helicopter and the Mi-2U dual control training variant. Standard Mil Mi-2s had only one pilot's seat, mounted on the left, with no position for a co-pilot. In the utility role, the Mi-2 could carry eight passengers plus the pilot in its air-conditioned cabin. A winch could be fitted for SAR duties with a capacity of 150kg (330lb), and when used for the medevac role, four stretchers and a medical attendant could be carried.

Deliveries to the Soviet military began in 1965, and this unpretentious, reliable and useful helicopter proved popular. Examples were supplied to all the Warsaw Pact nations as well as a host of Soviet client states, many of which are still flying.

Mi-2

This helicopter was operated in Aeroflot markings by the Science Academy Research Unit at Moscow, Sheremetyavo in 1992. It is preserved in Germany at Cämmerswalde Flugzeugmuseum.

Mil Mi-2 'Hoplite'

Weight (maximum take-off): 3700kg (8157lb)
Dimensions: Length 17.42m (57ft 2in), Rotor diameter 14.5m (47ft 8in), Height 3.75m (12ft 4in)
Powerplant: Two 450kW (604shp) Klimov GTD-350P turboshaft engines
Maximum speed: 200km/h (120mph)
Range: 440km (270 miles)
Ceiling: 4000m (13,000ft)
Crew: 1–2
Maximum payload: 700kg (1543lb) internally or 800kg (1764lb) as a slung load

HELICOPTERS

Mil Mi-8 'Hip'

More Mil Mi-8s have been built than any other helicopter, and it has been in serial production constantly from 1964 to the present. The type remains in service with dozens of nations in both military and civilian roles.

The Mi-8 was designed as a turbine-powered successor to the mass-produced Mi-4 and was initially flown in single-engine form as the V-8 on 24 June 1961. The V-8 was hurriedly constructed, utilizing the rotor system and tail boom from the standard Mi-4, before it was displayed at the Tushino air show in July, the new helicopter received the reporting name Hip. The V-8 became the sole Hip-A when a second version, the V-8A, referred to as Hip-B by NATO, was flown on 17 September with a twin-turbine powerplant adopted primarily to improve safety in the event of engine failure. Further prototypes followed, introducing the distinctive five-bladed rotor and tailored to both military assault, as the V-8AT, and VIP transport, as the V-8AP.

During trials, the V-8A demonstrated the ability to lift twice the payload of the Mi-4 and to fly half as fast again as the older helicopter, at the same time proving considerably more economical to operate. The first production aircraft was the Mi-8T utility transport, built in Kazan, which first appeared in late 1964; the Mi-8P heli-liner following in 1965 and both received the Hip-C NATO reporting name. Demand was such that a second production line was launched at Ulan-Ude in 1970. There followed a bewildering number of variants adapted for virtually every purpose a helicopter could realistically be used for.

Armed version

The initial Mi-8T military version had been intended to carry armament from the start, but armed versions did not appear until 1968. Fitted with weapon outriggers from the earlier Mi-4AV and later designated Mi-8TV, a typical load consisted of four 16-round 57mm (2.24in) unguided rocket pods. Bombs up to 500kg (1100lb) each could be carried instead, and the lower forward nose window could be replaced with a panel incorporating a mount for a 7.62mm (0.3in) PKT machine gun.

An improved variant, informally designated the Mi-8TV-2, appeared in 1974, featuring a new armament system with three stores racks on each outrigger, instead of the previous two; it was capable of carrying heavier loads including, for the first time, 9M17P Falanga-P radio-guided anti-tank missiles.

Mi-8T

'59 Red' is shown as it appeared during Waffenbrüderschaft 80, a major military exercise to commemorate 25 years of the Warsaw Pact. The exercise included a simulated amphibious assault on the beach at Peenemünde/Karlshagen in East Germany.

Mil Mi-8T

Weight (maximum take-off): 12,000kg (26,455lb)
Dimensions: Length 18.17m (59ft 7in), Rotor diameter 21.29m (69ft 10in), Height 5.65m (18ft 1in)
Powerplant: Two 1268kW (1700shp) Klimov TV3-117A turboshaft engines
Maximum speed: 250km/h (160mph)
Range: 350km (217 miles)
Ceiling: 4500m (14,764ft)
Crew: 3
Armament: One optional 7.62mm (0.5in) PK machine gun, flexibly mounted on door mount; up to 4000kg (8800lb) of bombs, missiles and stores

Further military derivatives of the basic Mi-8 included the Mi-8VKP airborne command post (Hip-D), featuring an extensive array of antennae – most conspicuously, twin outward-canted "towel rack" antennae above the fuselage. This variant also mounted equipment boxes permanently fitted to the stores outriggers. The Mi-8IV (Hip-G)

HELICOPTERS

of the late 1970s was also a tactical airborne command post variant and dispensed with the external stores but did feature long strake antennae under the fuselage. ECM variants were also produced: the Mi-8MV (Hip-J) carried the *Smalt'a-V* system to jam enemy defence radars, and the Mi-8PP (Hip-K) also carried jamming equipment but was equipped to perform SIGINT functions as well. Each side of the fuselage carried a boxy fairing under the rotor, and a rectangular array of six X-shaped antennas were fitted to the tailboom. Heat exchangers were fitted in fairings in a lateral row underneath the fuselage to deal with the excess heat generated by all this equipment.

Variants

In addition to these roles, Mi-8s were developed for the medevac role as the Mi-8MB, and as aerial minelayers, the Mi-8AV and Mi-8AD were used to sow anti-tank and anti-personnel mines respectively. The Mi-8R was a battlefield reconnaissance variant, and a subtype specifically developed for radiation on a nuclear battlefield appeared as the Mi-8VD. The Mi-8TARK was optimized for artillery spotting, and Mi-8s have also been used as a fuel tanker intended to refuel ground transport, other helicopters (designated the Mi-8TZ) and a firefighting machine, the Mi-8TL, with a large bucket carried as an underslung load. Additionally, many one-off trials and experimental Mi-8s were produced, and the helicopter even managed to set a speed record for its class when a modified Mi-8T achieved 273km/h (170mph) flown by an all-woman crew.

Second generation

A second generation of Mi-8 started to be built in 1977, featuring new TV3-117MT engines of greater power, originally developed for the Mi-14, along with an improved transmission to handle the extra power and numerous other internal improvements. Designated the Mi-8MT (Hip-H), these uprated Mi-8s can be easily identified by the tail rotor being placed on the left-hand side of the tail boom rather than the right. Production of first- and second-generation Hips overlapped with the earlier design being produced until 1986.

Further improvements to the Mi-8 were incorporated into production machines as a result of combat experience in Afghanistan, with efforts to improve the 'hot and high' performance of the aircraft coupled with improvements to the self-defence weapons carried being of paramount importance. As a result, later Soviet Mi-8s featured intake dust filters and two or four PKT machine guns, which could be fitted to the outriggers. Some were fitted with a 12.7mm (0.50in) NSV-12.7 *Utyos* ('Cliff') machine gun or a 30mm (1.18in) *Plamya* ('Flame') automatic grenade launcher on mountings in the side door and rear hatch. Vulnerability to MANPADS, such as the Stinger, saw filters to mask exhaust heat with cool air fitted to machines built from 1984. Chaff-flare dispensers were also added.

Still in full production when the Cold War came to an end, over 17,000 examples of the Mi-8 had been built by 2024. Production of improved models has occurred since 1992, and many upgrades have kept earlier models viable as military aircraft until the present day. Thousands of Mi-8s – both those built as civilian helicopters and others retired from military use – also remain flying in civilian hands across the world.

Mi-8MT

'12 Red' of the 2nd squadron of the 335th Independent Helicopter Regiment was based at Jalalabad, Afghanistan, in 1981. This aircraft lacks most of the self-defence systems added following operational experience, although flare dispensers are fitted under the tail boom.

Mil Mi-8MT

Weight (maximum take-off): 13,000kg (28,660lb)
Dimensions: Length 18.4m (60ft 4in), Rotor diameter 21.29m (69ft 10in), Height 5.5m (18ft 1in)
Powerplant: Two 1454kW (1950shp) Klimov TV3-117MT turboshaft engines
Maximum speed: 250km/h (160mph)
Range: 495km (308 miles)
Ceiling: 5000m (16,000ft)
Crew: 3
Armament: One optional 7.62mm (0.5in) PK machine gun, flexibly mounted on door mount; up to 4000kg (8800lb) of bombs, missiles and stores

HELICOPTERS
Mil Mi-14 'Haze'

An amphibious development of the ubiquitous Mi-8, the Mi-14 added a boat-like hull and was intended for anti-submarine warfare duties.

The Mi-14 answered a Naval Aviation requirement for a helicopter to replace the Mi-4M in the coastal anti-submarine warfare role, the older helicopter having been seen as a stopgap solution from the start. Mil began work on the V-8G, derived from the Mi-8, as early as 1959, though detail design work did not begin until 1962.

The helicopter was initially intended to operate as either a 'hunter' or 'killer', as it was felt that a single airframe would be unable to carry both the search equipment necessary to locate enemy submarines and the armament to destroy them, but the power available from the TV3-117 engine by 1965 meant both tasks could be accomplished by the same helicopter, dubbed the V-14.

The V-14 made its maiden flight on 1 August 1967, and production of the Mi-14 began in 1969. However, service entry only took place in 1976, as both the offensive avionics suite and engines encountered developmental problems that took considerable time to iron out. In its standard ASW form, the Mi-14 (Haze-A) carried dipping sonar, 36 sonobuoys and an APM-20 *Orsha* towed magnetic anomaly detector as well as an *Initziativa-2M* surface search radar, all linked to an onboard analogue computer system.

A minesweeping variant, the Mi-14BT (Haze-B), utilized a towed sled for mine clearing, and a dedicated search-and-rescue variant called the Mi-14PS (Haze-C) was also produced, as well as conversions for passenger use and firefighting.

Although produced in a fraction of the numbers of its Mi-8 progenitor, with just 273 built between 1969 and 1986, in 2024, the Mi-14 remained in operational service with eight nations.

Mil Mi-14PS
Weight (maximum take-off): 14,000kg (30,865lb)
Dimensions: Length 18.38m (60ft 4in), Rotor diameter 21.29m (69ft 10in), Height 6.93m (22ft 9in)
Powerplant: Two 1454kW (1950shp) Klimov TV3-117M turboshaft engines
Maximum speed: 230km/h (143mph)
Range: 1200km (746 miles)
Ceiling: 4000m (13123ft)
Crew: 4
Maximum payload: Up to 3000kg (6600lb)

Mi-14PS
'02 Red' of the Independent Search and Rescue Squadron was based at Gorodskoy in Kazakhstan during 1984. At that time, Soviet search-and-rescue helicopters wore this scheme, incorporating a large orange lightning bolt across the upper fuselage.

Mil Mi-24 'Hind'

An aircraft synonymous with the tactical might of the Red Army, the distinctive Mi-24 has seen near-constant combat use from the Ogaden War of 1977 to the invasion of Ukraine in 2022.

The origins of the 'Hind' date to the early 1960s, by which time it had become clear that ever-improving battlefield mobility would require an airborne vehicle that could both provide tactical fire support and carry infantry into battle. Reports of helicopter operations by the US in Vietnam also convinced Soviet planners of the value of purpose-designed armed helicopters providing ground support. Mil revealed the mock-up of a helicopter designated V-24 in 1966 and flew the first prototype on 19 September 1969.

Based on the Mi-8's engine and transmission system, the Mi-24 featured a fuselage with armour protection, an Afanasev 12.7mm (0.5in) machine gun in the nose, along with sensors and anti-tank missile equipment, stub wings to carry stores and provide lift in forward flight and a retractable undercarriage. The pilot, navigator, and gunner occupied a heavily glazed cockpit, and eight troops could be seated back-to-back in two rows of four in the cabin.

Alternatively, the Mi-24 could carry four stretchers and an attendant, although in practice, both this capability and indeed the ability to carry troops has rarely been used. However, the cabin has proved useful for transporting its own service crew and equipment on remote detachments.

Into service

Acceptance testing began in June 1970, utilizing 10 pre-production machines, and continued for 18 months, with the first production aircraft appearing in 1971. The type was officially commissioned into service as the Mi-24A in 1972. From the start, the Mi-24 was fast, with much attention having been paid to the streamlining, and a lightened Mi-24B, designated the A-10, was used in 1978 to set the absolute speed record for helicopters at 368.4km/h (228.9mph), a record that would stand until 1986. Production Mi-24As were the first to be observed by the West and were therefore designated Hind-A. The pre-production aircraft were discovered later and confusingly dubbed Hind-B. The principal external difference between the two types is the stub wings, with a 12-degree anhedral added to the production Mi-24A to improve yaw stability.

Mi-24

Based at Stendal air base in East Germany in 1978, '03 White' was on the strength of 178 Assault and Combat Helicopter Regiment (OBVP). An example of the initial 'Hind-A', the aircraft is fitted with the original unstepped cockpit glazing.

Mil Mi-24 'Hind'

Weight (maximum take-off): 12,000kg (26,455lb)
Dimensions: Length 17.5m (57ft 5in), Rotor diameter 17.3m (56ft 9in), Height 6.5m (21ft 4in)
Powerplant: Two 1600kW (2200shp) Klimov TV3-117 turboshaft engines
Maximum speed: 320km/h (200mph)
Range: 450km (280 miles)
Ceiling: 4950m (16,240ft)
Crew: 3
Armament: One 12.7mm (0.5in) A-12.7 machine gun flexibly mounted in nose; up to 1275kg (2811lb) bombs, missiles, rockets or stores
Maximum payload: Up to 1500kg (3300lb) or 2000kg (4400lb) on external sling

Mi-24D

Only around 240 Mi-24A were built, as it had demonstrated a number of deficiencies in service. The main problems were that firepower was inadequate, crew protection was insufficient, and despite the extensive glazing of the cockpit, visibility was

HELICOPTERS

poor. A complete revision of the forward fuselage saw the crew reduced to two, and separate, heavily armoured cockpits were provided for them, gunner in front and pilot behind. The rotors were reinforced with titanium, allowing them to withstand hits from 20mm (0.79in) cannon, and armament was improved with a four-barrelled Yakoushev-Borzov YakB-12.7 12.7mm (0.5in) machine gun fitted in a nose turret. Usually operated by the gunner in the front seat, the gun could also be fixed to fire forward and aimed by the pilot through a gunsight. The stub wings were strengthened to handle heavier payloads and plumbed to allow external fuel tanks to be carried.

Improvements to the *Falanga* antitank missile in its Falanga-P AT-2 form saw its range increased and targeting simplified, raising the probability of a 'kill' from 30 per cent to over 80 per cent. Designated the Mi-24D, Hind-D, prototypes converted from Mi-24As were flying in 1972, and production began in 1973, with 550 having been delivered by the time production switched to the Mi-24V Hind-E. The Mi-24V was an update of the -24D, externally almost indistinguishable, which incorporated the advanced 9M114 *Sturm-V* tube-launched anti-tank missile, which was faster and longer ranged than the AT-2, whilst delivering a kill ratio of over 90 per cent.

Mi-24V

The Mi-24V became the most-produced Hind variant, with around 1500 produced for about a decade from 1976. Other improvements introduced with the Hind-E included stowable flight controls, added to the gunner's cockpit for emergency or training purposes, a head-up display (HUD) for the pilot, and improved avionics and uprated engines for better 'hot and high' performance following exposure to such conditions in Afghanistan. Experience in that country also led to the creation of the Mi-24P Hind-F, which introduced improved avionics but more dramatically included a fixed, forward-firing, twin-barrelled GSh-30K cannon in a fairing on the starboard side of

Cockpit
The heavily glazed cockpit of the Hind-A (known as the "veranda" to Soviet Mi-24 crews) was replaced from the Mi-24D onwards with this tandem design. Each position features a bulletproof windscreen and the separate crew stations conferred greater survivability than the earlier common-cockpit arrangement.

Rockets
This Hind is pictured launching S-5 rockets from its four UB-32 launchers. As the designation implies, each UB-32 is loaded with 32 rockets. The S-5 was developed from the World War II-era German R4M rocket for attacking area targets on the ground, though anti-armour, fragmentation and incendiary rounds were all developed.

the fuselage, with local strengthening to handle the considerable recoil of this weapon. The large size of the cannon precluded it being fitted in an undernose turret, and so it was aimed by pointing the entire helicopter at the target. In production from 1981, 620 examples were built. Although the 30mm (1.18in) cannon proved effective, its fixed fitting was less than ideal and led to the production of a compromise, the Mi-24VP, which had a 23mm (0.9in) GSh-23L cannon in a nose turret. Designed in 1985, only 24 examples of this Hind variant were built before the Soviet Union collapsed, and it never received a separate NATO designation.

As with other Soviet helicopters, several one-offs and specialist variants were built in small numbers before the end of the Cold War, and the Hind has remained in production in Russia from 1991 until the present day, becoming one of the most widely exported combat aircraft ever built and serving in nearly half of all countries that possess an armed air force. A staggering 74 nations have operated the Hind since 1972, with 58 countries retaining it in service in 2024.

Mil Mi-24D

Weight (maximum take-off): 12,000kg (26,455lb)
Dimensions: Length 17.48m (57ft 4in), Rotor diameter 17.2m (56 ft 7in), Height 6.4m (21ft 3in)
Powerplant: Two 1600kW (2200shp) Klimov TV3-117 turboshaft engines
Maximum speed: 335km/h (208mph)
Range: 750km (466 miles)
Ceiling: 4495m (14,750ft)
Crew: 3
Armament: Four 12.7mm (0.5in) YakB-12.7 Gatling machine gun in remotely controlled under-nose turret; up to 2400kg (5291lb) bombs, missiles or rockets
Maximum payload: Up to 1500kg (3300lb) or 2000kg (4400lb) on external sling

Mi-24D
Designed as a more specialised gunship than previous variants the Mi-24D began to reach combat units in 1976. This example was serving with the Soviet 16th Air Army in the German Democratic Republic in the early 1980s.

Passenger compartment
The Mi-24 could carry up to eight armed infantrymen in the rear compartment, the windows of which could be opened and a machine gun support was mounted at their base. The cockpit and rear compartment were both pressurised for protection against NBC fallout and as an alternative, it was possible to carry two stretchers and medical equipment.

HELICOPTERS

Mil Mi-26 'Halo'

The world's largest production helicopter, the enormous Mi-26 offers a capability as yet unmatched by any other VTOL aircraft worldwide.

Designed to replace the Mi-6 and Mi-10, the Mi-26 was intended to answer a need for a heavy-lift helicopter for both military and civil use. Flown for the first time on 14 December 1977, the first production helicopter was rolled out in October 1980, and the Mi-26 entered military service in 1983. In 1982, the Mil Mi-26 set the world record for the greatest mass lifted by a helicopter to 2000m (6562ft) by lifting 56,767.8kg (125,000lb) to that altitude, a record that still stands.

Heavy carrier

Despite weighing only slightly more than the Mi-6, the Mi-26 can carry nearly double the payload of the older helicopter, including up to 100 troops or 60 stretchers plus medical staff. Loading is through the hydraulically actuated clamshell doors and ramp at the rear of the fuselage, and a roller conveyor and two rail-mounted 2.5 tonne (5500lb) capacity winches are provided to move payloads within the cargo bay. The Mi-26 is the only helicopter in the world to utilize an eight-bladed main rotor.

The Mi-26 has proved highly effective in operational service, which began during the conflict in Afghanistan. In 1986, 30 Mi-26s were used for precision drops of insulating material to cover the damaged No. 4 reactor at Chernobyl, and the helicopter has subsequently become prized for its unique load-carrying ability. Post-Soviet use has seen the Mi-26 used to transport a 23,000-year-old woolly mammoth encased in a 23 tonne (50,700lb) block of frozen soil and to recover two US Army MH-47 Chinook helicopters in Afghanistan, as there was no American helicopter that could accomplish the task. Over 300 have been built since production began in 1980, and the helicopter remains in production in 2024 at Rostvertol.

Mil Mi-26 'Halo'

Weight (maximum take-off): 56,000kg (123,459lb)
Dimensions: Length 40.03m (131ft 4in), Rotor diameter 32m (105ft), Height 8.15m (26ft 9in)
Powerplant: Two 8500kW (11400shp) Lotarev D-136 turboshaft engines
Maximum speed: 295km/h (183mph)
Range: 1920km (1190 miles)
Ceiling: 4600m (15,100ft)
Crew: 5
Maximum payload: 20,000kg (44,092lb)

Mi-26

'60 Yellow' from 4th squadron of the 276th Independent Combat Helicopter Regiment (276 OVP), subordinated to the 5th Independent Guards Army Corps, based at Borovukha-1 (Novopolosk, Belarus) in May 1986. This aircraft was one of several deployed to the Chernobyl nuclear reactor site, following the explosion of its Number Four reactor. Hastily fitted with improvised lead lining in the cabin, the crews, nonetheless, operated under extremely hazardous conditions, spraying adhesive liquid in an effort to bind the highly radioactive dust, or dumping sand and lead directly onto the reactor itself. Once the immediate emergency had been contained, the helicopters used for these missions were abandoned close to the plant, as they had become dangerously radioactive and many of the crews involved later suffered serious health issues.

Index

Page numbers in *italics* refer to illustration captions

3M11 Falanga missile 108
7.62mm (0.3in) PKT machine gun 118
9M14 Malyutka missile 108
9M17M Falanga missile *109*
9M17P Falanga-P missile 118, 122
9M114 *Sturm-V* tube-launched antitank missile 122
12.7mm (0.5in) A-12.7 machine gun 109
12.7mm (0.5in) NSV-12.7 *Utyos* ('Cliff') machine-gun 119
20mm (0.79in) Berezin B-20 cannon 48
23mm (0.9in) guns *12*, 18, 24, 62, 68
23mm (0.9in) AM-23 cannon 94
23mm (0.9in) Nudelman-Suranov NS-23 cannon 23, 48
30mm (1.18in) NR-30 cannon 23, 24, 27
30mm (1.18in) *Plamya* ('Flame') automatic grenade launcher 119
37mm (1.46in) NL-37L cannon 12, 16, 18, 25
57mm (2.24in) NAR S-5M rocket 109, 118
212mm (8.3in) ARS-212 unguided rocket 25

AA-2 missile 27
AA-11 Archer *44*
Abłamowicz, Andrzej 14
Admiral Kuznetsov (carrier) 43, 58
Aero S-105 24
Aero S-106 27
Afanasev 12.7mm (0.5in) machine gun 121
Afghanistan *39*, 51, 56, 63, 72, 75, 87, 95, 100, 101, 124
Albania 110
Algeria 37, 53
Angola 100
Antarctic 105, *110*
Antonov An-2 'Colt' 80
Antonov An-8 'Camp' 93
  DT-5/8 93
Antonov An-12 'Cub' 94–5
  An-10 ('Cab') 94
  An-12A 94
  An-12AP 95
  An-12B 94
  An-12BK 95
  An-12BP 95
  An-12P 95
  Shaaxi Y-8 95
Antonov An-22 'Cock' *90–1*, 100
Antonov An-24 'Coke' 96–7
  An-24PRT 96
  An-24RR 96
  An-24RT 96
  An-24S 96
  An-24ShT 96
  An-24T 96, 97
Antonov An-26 'Curl' 98–9
  An-26RT 98
  An-26RTR 98
  An-26S 98
  An-26Sh 98
  An-26 *Shtabnoy* 98
  An-26T 99

Antonov An-30 'Clank' 96–7
Antonov An-32 'Cline' 98–9
Antonov An-72 and An-74 'Coaler' 105
  An-71 'Madcap' 105
Antonov An-124 'Condor' 104
Arctic 24, 81, 92, 98, 105
AS-1 *Kometa* 66
Avia B-33 48
Azerbaijan 80

Belarus 43, *72, 73, 124*
Belenko, Viktor 36, 37
Beriev A-50 102–3
Beriev Be-6 'Madge' *78–9*, 81
Beriev Be-10 'Mallow' 82
Beriev Be-12 'Mail' 84
  Be-12PS 84
Biafran conflict 63
Black Sea *10*, 64, 82, 84
Boeing B-29 Superfortress 18, 62
Boeing RB-47H 24
Bulgaria 115
BVR missile 38

Canada 116
Chad 73
Chechnya 75
Chengdu J-7 and F-7 27, 30
Chernobyl nuclear disaster 97, 124, *124*
China 72, 74
  attack aircraft 48
  bombers 62, 63, *63*, 64, 66
  Civil War 17
  fighters 11, *16*, 17, 18, 19, 21, 22, 24, 27, 30, 43
  flying boat 81
  helicopters 110
  transport aircraft 94, 95
  utility 80
Croatia 80
Cuba *23, 24*
Czechoslovakia
  aircraft of *7*, 14, *18*, 19, 24, 27, *28*, 30, 48, 58, 95
  Soviet invasion of *20, 30*, 93, 95

East Germany *7, 21, 22, 29, 35*, 44, *45, 55, 57, 99, 121*
Egypt 22, 36, 50, 63, 66, 100
Ethiopia 100

FAB-250 bomb 23
Finland *44*
Focke-Wulf Ta 183 16

Gagarin, Yuri *19*
Georgia 75
gliders 92
GSh-6-30 30mm (1.18in) weapon 55
GSh-30K cannon 122–3
GShL-23 23mm (0.9in) cannon 29
Gulf War 51, 53

Harbin H-5 63
Harbin Z-5 110

Ilyushin Il-10 'Beast' 48
  Avia B-33 48
Ilyushin Il-18 87–8
  Coot-B 88
  Il-18D 88
  Il-18S 87
Ilyushin Il-20 87–8
  Il-20M 88
Ilyushin Il-22 'Coot' 87–8
  Il-22M 88
  Il-22PP 88
Ilyushin Il-28 'Beagle' *7*, 63
  Il-28N 63
  Il-28R 63
  Il-28T 63
  Il-28U (Mascot) 63
Ilyushin Il-38 'May' 87–8
  Il-38 ASW 87–8
Ilyushin Il-76 'Candid' 101–3
  Il-76M 101
  Il-76MD 101, 102, 103
  Il-76TD 102
Ilyushin Il-78 'Midas' 101–3
  Il-78 102
  Il-82 102
Ilyushin Il-80 'Maxdome' 89
  Il-86 Camber 89
India 28, 29, 30, 37, 50, 55, 88, 99, 101, 115
Iran 37, 51, 53, 66, 73
Iraq 22, 37, 51, 53, 66, 73
Israel 29, 36, 63, 66

Japan 36, 37, 48, 62
Jordan 22

K-5 beam-riding missile 31
K-10S missile 65, 66, *66–7*
K-13 missile 29, 72
K-14S stand-off missile 70
Kamov Ka-10 'Hat' 114
Kamov Ka-15 'Hen' 114
Kamov Ka-25 'Hormone' 114–15
  Ka-25BShZ 115
  Ka-25F 115
  Ka-25K 115
  Ka-25PL Hormone-A 114
  Ka-25PS Hormone-C 114–15
  Ka-25T Hormone-B 114
Kamov Ka-27 115–16
  Ka-27PL 115–16
  Ka-27PS 116
Kamov Ka-28 116
Kamov Ka-29 'Helix' 115–16
Kamov Ka-31 116
Kamov Ka-32 116
Kargil War (1999) 37
Kazakhstan 55, *120*
Kh-10 missile *70*
Kh-15 missile 74, *75*, 76
Kh-20 missile 69
Kh-22 missile 69, 73, 74, *75*
Kh-55 missile 69, 76
Kh-55SM missile 69
Kh-101 missile 76
Khruschev, Nikita 73, 74

INDEX

Korean Airlines crash (1983) 34
Korean War (1950–3) 10, 11, *16*, 17, 18, 48, 80
Kozhedub, Ivan 11
KS-1 *Kometa* 66
KSR missile 66, *70*

Lavochkin La-9 and La-11 'Fritz' 11
Lavochkin La-15 'Fantai' 15
Lavochkin La-160 15
Libya 53, 66, 73, 101
Lockheed U-2 24

Mao Zedong 17
Mikoyan-Gurevich MiG-9 'Fargo' 12
Mikoyan-Gurevich MiG-15 'Fagot' 6, *8*, 15, 16–19
   I-310 16–17
   JJ-2 19
   Lim-1 and Lim-2 19
   MiG-15bis 16, 17
   MiG-15UTI 17, 18, 19
   S-102 and S-103 19
   SBLim-1 and -2 19
Mikoyan-Gurevich MiG-17 'Fresco' *6*, 20–2
   F-5 21
   I-330 'SI' 20
   Lim-5 and Lim-5P 21
   Lim-5M 21
   Lim-6bis 21
   MiG-17F 20–1, 22
   MiG-17P 20
   MiG-17PF 21, 22
   MiG-17UTI 22
   Shenyang J-5 21
   Shenyang JJ-5 22
Mikoyan-Gurevich MiG-19 'Farmer' 23–4
   Aero S-105 24
   F-6 24
   Farmer-A 23
   JJ-6 24
   MiG-19P Farmer-B 23–4
   MiG-19S Farmer-C 23, 24
   MiG-19SV 24
   Q-5 24
   Shenyang J-6 24
Mikoyan-Gurevich MiG-21 'Fishbed' 27–30
   Aero S-106 27
   Chengdu J-7 and F-7 27, 30
   MiG-21bis Fishbed-L 30
   MiG-21bis Fishbed-N 30
   MiG-21F-13 Fishbed-C 27, 29
   MiG-21F Fishbed-B 27
   MiG-21MF 30
   MiG-21P Fishbed-D 28
   MiG-21PF Fishbed-F 27, 28
   MiG-21PFM Fishbed-F 28
   MiG-21PFMA Fishbed-J 28
   MiG-21R Fishbed-H 28–9
   MiG-21S Fishbed-H 29
   MiG-21SM 29–30, 30
   MiG-21SMT Fishbed-K 30
   MiG-21U, US and UM Mongol 30
Mikoyan-Gurevich MiG-23 'Flogger' 38–9
   MiG-23B Flogger-F 39
   MiG-23M Flogger-B 38
   MiG-23MF 38, 39
   MiG-23ML 39

MiG-23MLA Flogger-G 39
MiG-23MLD Flogger-K 39
MiG-23MS 39
MiG-23P Flogger-L 39
MiG-23S Flogger-A 38
MiG-23U Flogger-C 39
MiG-23UB Flogger-C 39
Ye-231 38
Mikoyan-Gurevich MiG-25 'Foxbat' 35–7
   Foxbat-C 36
   MiG- 25P Foxbat-A 36–7
   MiG-25PD Foxbat-E 36–7
   MiG-25R Foxbat-B 36, 37
   MiG-25RBM 35
Mikoyan-Gurevich MiG-27 'Flogger' 54–5
   MiG-23 54
   MiG-23B Flogger-F 54
   MiG-23BM 54
   MiG-23BN Flogger-H 54, 55
   MiG-23M 55
   MiG-23Sh 54
   MiG-27 Flogger-D 55
   MiG-27K Flogger-J2 55
   MiG-27M Flogger-J 55
Mikoyan-Gurevich MiG-31 'Foxhound' 41
   MIG-25MP 41
   MiG-31M Foxhound-B 41
Mikoyan MiG-29 'Fulcrum' 44–5
   Fulcrum-A 44
   Fulcrum-C 44, 45
   MiG-29K 45
   MiG-29S 45
   MiG-29SMT 45
   MiG-29UB Fulcrum-B 45
   MiG-35 45
Mil Mi-1 'Hare' 108
   GM-1 108
   Mi-1 *Moskvich* 108
   Mi-1MU 108
   Mi-1T 108
   Mi-1U 108
   SM-1 108
   SM-2 108
Mil Mi-2 'Hoplite' 117
   Mi-2U 117
Mil Mi-4 'Hound' 109–10
   Harbin Z-5 110
   Mi-4A Hound-A 109
   Mi-4AV 109
   Mi-4BT 109
   Mi-4KK 109
   Mi-4KU 109
   Mi-4L 109
   Mi-4M Hound-B 109
   Mi-4MK 109
   Mi-4PL Hound-C 109
   Mi-4PS 109
   Mi-4T 109
   Mi-4U 109
   Mi-4UM 109
Mil Mi-6 'Hook' 112–13
   Mi-6A 113
   Mi-6APS 113
   Mi-6PS 113
   Mi-6PZh2 113
   Mi-6T 113
   Mi-6TZ 113
Mi-10 'Harke' 112–13

Mi-10PP 112–13
Mil Mi-8 'Hip' *106*–7, 118–19
   Mi-8AD 119
   Mi-8AV 119
   Mi-8IV Hip-G 118–19
   Mi-8MB 119
   Mi-8MT 119
   Mi-8MT Hip-H 119
   Mi-8MV Hip-J 119
   Mi-8P Hip-C 118
   Mi-8PP Hip-K 119
   Mi-8R 119
   Mi-8T Hip-C 118, 119
   Mi-8TARK 119
   Mi-8TL 119
   Mi-8TV 118
   Mi-8TV-2 118
   Mi-8TZ 119
   Mi-8VD 119
   Mi-8VKP Hip-D 118
   V-8 118
   V-8A Hip-B 118
   V-8AP 118
   V-8AT 118
Mil Mi-14 'Haze' 120
   Mi-14 Haze-A 120
   Mi-14BT Haze-B 120
   Mi-14PS Haze-C 120
   V-14 120
Mil Mi-24 'Hind' 121–3
   Hind-B 121
   Mi-24A Hind-A 121, *122*
   Mi-24B (A-10) 121
   Mi-24D Hind-D 121–3
   Mi-24P Hind-F 122–3
   Mi-24V Hind-E 122
   Mi-24VP 123
   V-24 121
Mil Mi-26 'Halo' 124
Myasishchev M-4 and 3M 'Bison' 70
   3M Bison-B 70
   3MD Bison-C 70
   M-4 Bison-A 70
   VM-T *Atlant* ('Atlas') freighters 70

Nagorno-Karabakh War (2020) 80
Nguyen Van Coc 29
Nigeria 22, 63
North American F-86 Sabre 18, 20
North Korea 10, 11, 18, 19, 22, 63, 80, 110
North Vietnam 21, 23
   see also Vietnam War
North Yemen Civil War (1963) 22, 63
Nudelman-Richter NR-23 cannon 17, *94*
Nudelman-Richter NR-30 30mm (1.18in) cannon 49
Nudelman-Suranov NS-23 23mm (0.9in) cannon 16, *63*

Operation Parakram 37
ORO-32K unguided rocket 23

P-6 missile *70*
Pakistan 29, 37, 50
Pepelyayev, Yevgeny *16*
Peru 59, 100
Poland 14, *15*, 19, 21, *35, 42*, 51, 80, 95, 108, 117

INDEX

Powers, Gary 24

R-3R (K-13R) missile 29
R-4 missile 32, *32*
R-4R missile 32
R-4RM missile 32
R-4T missile 32
R-4TM missile 32
R-8/K-8 missile 33
R-8M-1 missile 72
R-23 missile 39
R-27R missile 45
R-27RE/TE missile 45
R-27T missile 45
R-33 missile 41
R-33S missile 41
R-40 missile 36
R-40TD missile 41
R-60 missile 30, 34, 37, 39
R-60M missile 30, 41, 45
R-73 missile *44*, 45
R-77 missile 45
R-98 missile 31, 33
R-98MR missile 31
R-98MT infrared-guided 31
RAT-52 rocket propelled torpedo 63
RDS-3 atomic bomb 62
Romania 14, *22*, 30
Russia (post break-up of the USSR) 7
   attack aircraft *50*, 53, 55, 59
   bombers 68, 73, 75, 76
   fighters 34, 39, 41, 43, 45
   helicopters 115, 123, 124
   invasion of Ukraine 75, 80, 88, 101
   reconnaissance, electronic warfare & utility 80, 86, 87, 88
   transport aircraft 95, 100, 101, *103*, 105

S-5 rockets *122*
Shaaxi Y-8 95
Shenyang J-5 21
Shenyang J-6 24
Shenyang JJ-5 22
Six Day War (1967) 22, 63
South Korea 48, 116
Soviet Armed Forces (PVO, VVS, AV-MF) 7
   5th Independent Guards Army Corps *124*
   6th Guards Fighter Aviation Regiment *10*
   12th Independent Helicopter Regiment *112*
   16th Air Army *123*
   31st Guards Fighter Regiment *45*
   83th Anti-Submarine Warfare Regiment *115*
   121st Guards Sevastopol Red Banner Heavy Bomber Regiment *72*
   178th Assault and Combat Helicopter Regiment (OBVP) *121*
   184th Guards Heavy Bomber Aviation Regiment *76*
   201st Heavy Bomber Aviation Division *76*
   234th Guards Fighter Aviation Regiment *44*
   276th Independent Combat Helicopter Regiment *124*
   290th Guards Long Range Aviation Regiment *73*
   335th Independent Helicopter Regiment *119*
   582nd Fighter Aviation Regiment *42*
   830th Independent Shipborne Anti-Submarine Helicopter Regiment *116*

   867th Independent Guards Long Range Reconnaissance Aviation Regiment *68*
   967th Long-Range Air Reconnaissance Regiment *66*
   977th Independent Naval Long-range Reconnaissance Air Regiment *82*
   Independent Search and Rescue Squadron *120*
Sri Lanka 22
Sudan 53
Sukhoi Su-7 'Fitter' 31, 49–50
   S-1 49
   S-2 49
   Su-7B Fitter-A 49–50
   Su-7BKL 50
   Su-7BM 50
   Su-7BMK 49, 50
   Su-7U 'Moujik' 50
   Su-7UMK 50
Sukhoi Su-9 and Su-11 'Fishpot' 31
   T-43 31
   T-431 31
Sukhoi Su-15 'Flagon' 33–4
   Flagon-A 33
   Flagon-D 33–4
   Flagon-F 34
   Su-15T 34
   Su-15TM Flagon-E 33, 34
   Su-15UM Flagon-G 34
   Su-15UT Flagon-C 34
   T-58 33
Sukhoi Su-17 and Sukhoi Su-22 'Fitter' 50–1
   Su-17M-4 50, 51
   Su-17M Fitter-C 51
   Su-17M2 Fitter-D 51
   Su-17M3 Fitter-H 51
   Su-17M4 Fitter-K 51
   Su-17UM Fitter-G 51
Sukhoi Su-24 'Fencer' 52–3
   Fencer-A 52
   Fencer-B 52
   Fencer-C *52*
   Su-24M Fencer-D 53
   Su-24MK 53
   Su-24MP Fencer-F 53
   Su-24MR Fencer-E 53
   T6-1 52
   T6-2I 52
Sukhoi Su-25 'Frogfoot' *46–7*, 56–9
   Su-25BM 57
   Su-25K 58
   Su-25T 58–9
   Su-25TM *58–9*
   Su-25UB Frogfoot-A 58
   Su-25UB Frogfoot-B 57–8
   Su-25UBK 58
   Su-25UTG 58
   T8 56
   T8-1 56
Sukhoi Su-27 'Flanker' 42–3
   J-11 43
   P-42 43
   Su-27K 42
   Su-27K Flanker-D 43
   Su-27P Flanker-B 43
   Su-27S 42
   Su-27S Flanker-B 43
   Su-27UB Flanker-C 43
   Su-30 43

Su-33 43
Su-34 43
Su-35 43
T-10 Flanker-A 42–3
T-10S 43
Sutyagin, Nikolay 18
Switzerland 116
Syria 22, 37, 39, 53, 69, 75, 76, 100, 115

Tanker War (1988) 73
Tbilisi (carrier) 43, 58
TKB-481 12.7mm (0.5in) machine gun 111
Tolkachev, Adolf *103*
Tupolev Tu-4 'Bull' 6, *60–1*, 62
Tupolev Tu-14 'Bosun' 64
Tu-14R 64
Tupolev Tu-16 'Badger' 65–7
   Tu-16 Badger-A *65*
   Tu-16A *65*
   Tu-16G *65*, 66
   Tu-16K-10 *65*
   Tu-16K-10 Badger-C 66–7
   Tu-16K Badger-G 66
   Tu-16KS Badger-B 66
   Tu-16KSR Badger-G 66
   Tu-16N 66
   Tu-16R Badger-E 66
   Tu-16RM-1 Badger-C 66
   Tu-16RM-2 Badger-F 66
   Tu-16S 66
   Tu-16T 66
   Tu-16Ye 66
   Xian H-6 66
Tupolev Tu-22 'Blinder' 72–3
   Tu-22B 73
   Tu-22K Blinder-B 73
   Tu-22PD 72
   Tu-22R Blinder-C 73
   Tu-22RDM Blinder C-2 73
   Tu-22U Blinder-D 73
Tupolev Tu-22M 'Backfire' 74–5
   T-4 74
   Tu-22M1 Backfire-A 74
   Tu-22M2 Backfire-B 74
   Tu-22M3 Backfire-C 74, 75
Tupolev Tu-95 'Bear' 68–9
   Tu-95 Bear-A 68
   Tu-95K-22 Bear-G 69
   Tu-95K Bear-B 69
   Tu-95KD Bear-B 69
   Tu-95MS Bear-H 69
   Tu-95RM Bear-E 69
   Tu-95RTS Bear-D *68*, 69
   Tu-95V 68
   Tu-142 69
Tupolev Tu-126 'Moss' 85
Tupolev Tu-128 'Fiddler' 32
   Tu-28 32
   Tu-28P *32*
   Tu-128M 32
   Tu-128UT 32
Tupolev Tu-142 'Bear' 86–7
   Bear-F 86
   Tu-142M 86
   Tu-142MK 87
   Tu-142MR Bear-J 87
   Tu-142MZ 87
Tupolev Tu-160 'Blackjack' 76–7

INDEX & PICTURE CREDITS

Ukraine 34, 43, 53, 59, 76, 84, 115
  invasion of 75, 80, 88, 101
United Kingdom 62
United States 11, 24, 56, 62
  bomber gap 70
  'Feather Duster' 21–2
  Vietnam War 21, 24, 29, 56, 80, 113
Uzbekistan 43

Vanya hydrogen bomb 68
Vietnam 115
Vietnam War (1955–75) 21, 24, 29, 56, 80, 113
Vympel K-13 missile 24

World War II 48

Xian H-6 66

Yakovlev Yak-9 'Frank' 10
  Yak-9P 10

Yak-9U 10
Yakovlev Yak-14 'Crow' 92
Yakovlev Yak-15 and Yak-17 'Feather' 13
  Yak-17UTI 'Magnet' 13
Yakovlev Yak-23 'Flora' 14–15
Yakovlev Yak-24 'Horse' 111
  Yak-24A 111
  Yak-24K 111
  Yak-24T 111
  Yak-24U 111
Yakovlev Yak-25 'Flashlight' and 'Mandrake' 25–6
  Yak-25M 25–6
  Yak-25R 26
  Yak-25RV 26
  Yak-120 25
Yakovlev Yak-27 'Mangrove' 83
  Flashlight-C 83
  Yak-27R 83
  Yak-27V 83

Yakovlev Yak-28 'Brewer' and 'Firebar' 71–2
  Yak-28B Brewer-A 71
  Yak-28I Brewer-C 71
  Yak-28L Brewer-B 71
  Yak-28P 'Firebar' 72
  Yak-28PP 71, 72
  Yak-28R Brewer-D 71–2
  Yak-28U (Maestro) 71
Yakovlev Yak-38 'Forger' 40
  Yak-36M 40
  Yak-38M 40
  Yak-38U 40
  Yak-141 'Freestyle' 40
Yemen 22, 63
Yom Kippur War (1973) 22, 63, 100
Yugoslavia 115

Picture Credits

PHOTOGRAPHS:

AirSeaLand Images: 6, 7, 8, 19, 60, 78, 81, 85, 106

Alamy: 62 (Corentin LE GALL), 77 (Associated Press)

Amber Books: 28

Creative Commons Attribution-Share Alike 2.0 Generic Licence: 15 (Alan Wilson)

Creative Commons Attribution-Share Alike 3.0 Imported Licence: 92

Getty Images: 90 (Evening Standard), 110 (Corbis)

Shutterstock: 26 (Aleks49), 46 (Vladislav Sinelnikov), 83 (CEPTAP)

ARTWORKS:

Amber Books: 10, 11, 32–39 all, 41, 44/45, 48–55 all, 57–59 all, 63, 66/67, 67, 70, 72, 75 both, 80, 82, 84, 86–88 all, 94, 95, 100, 102 both, 103 middle, 105, 109, 122/123

Teasel Studios: 5, 29 top, 44, 45, 68, 69, 71, 73, 74, 76/77, 108, 110–121 all, 124

Rolando Ugolini: 12–27 all, 29 bottom, 30, 31, 40 both, 42, 42/43, 56, 64–65 all, 89, 93, 96–99 all, 101, 103 top & bottom, 104